repentance and renewal

alba house
DIVISION OF THE SOCIETY OF ST. PAUL
STATEN ISLAND, N.Y. 10314

reflections on the
new liturgical readings for
the weekdays of lent

repentance
and renewal

Charles E. Miller, C.M.
John A. Grindel, C.M.

Current Printing (last digit):

9 8 7 6 5 4 3 2

Imprimi Potest:
   Joseph S. Falanga, C.M.
   Vice Provincial, Los Angeles Vice Province

Nihil Obstat:
   Patrick Dignan
   Censor Deputatus

Imprimatur:
   Timothy Manning
   Archbishop of Los Angeles
   August 28, 1970

The nihil obstat, imprimi potest and imprimatur are official declarations that a book or pamphlet is free of doctrinal or moral error. No implication is contained therein that those who have granted the nihil obstat and imprimatur agree with the contents, opinions or statements expressed.

Library of Congress Catalog Card Number: 70-148679

SBN: 8189-0212-4

Copyright 1971 by the Society of St. Paul, 2187 Victory Blvd., Staten Island, New York 10314

Designed, printed and bound in the U.S.A. by the Pauline Fathers and Brothers of the Society of St. Paul, 2187 Victory Blvd., Staten Island, N.Y. 10314 as part of their communications apostolate.

TABLE OF CONTENTS

INTRODUCTION

This book contains a short commentary on each of the lessons and gospels of the weekdays of Lent, as well as two brief reflections for each day. The commentaries have been composed in an objective fashion, without any attempt to relate the readings to each other or to the liturgy of Lent. The reflections are illustrations of how the scriptural material can be developed into a meditation or brief homily of about two minutes; they attempt to relate the lesson and gospel to each other when possible, and to turn the commentaries into material suitable for Lenten meditations or sermons.

The commentaries and reflections should be especially helpful in this connection to the preacher as he prepares his own personal homily for the day. We suggest, when used in this fashion, that the priest, deacon, or other suitable minister summarize the commentaries in a sentence or two; this summary may then be presented to the people either after the greeting or just before the readings.

Scriptural quotations are from the New American Version by members of the Catholic Biblical Association.

We sincerely hope and pray that this book will be a source of inspiration to many and an aid to the Lenten preacher, recognizing all the while that it can never substitute for one's own prayer, study, and creativity.

Charles E. Miller, C.M.
John A. Grindel, C.M.

St. John's Seminary
Camarillo, California

repentance and renewal

ASH WEDNESDAY

Joel 2, 12-18

The people are suffering from a great plague of locusts which the prophet sees as an anticipation and warning of the eschatological Day of the Lord. Therefore, the prophet calls on the people, in the name of the Lord, for a true repentance which must not be just an outward show but it must also include a sincere contrition, a real change of heart (vv. 12-13). Yahweh, being gracious and merciful, may forgive and revive their agricultural and pastoral prosperity so that they can again have something to sacrifice to him (13-14). All the people, even those who might think themselves dispensed, must be involved in this act of public penance and prayer (15-16). The motive presented to Yahweh for saving them is possible scandal: if he does not save, the gentiles may doubt his power to protect them. The Lord hears their prayer.

2 Corinthians 5, 20-6, 2

In 5, 20 Paul sums up the office of an apostle: he is a legate of Christ and an instrument of God. As a legate of Christ, Paul exhorts the Corinthians to be reconciled to God. He is here speaking of the final reconciliation, the definitive possession of eternal life, and thus, indirectly, he is exhorting them to be faithful now to God, with whom they have already been reconciled at baptism, and to return to Him if they have strayed. Such reconciliation is possible because Jesus, though without sin, was made a sacrifice for sin by the Father so that we, through our solidarity with Jesus, might be justified. Therefore, Paul exhorts them not to let this redemptive work of God through Christ go in vain. It would if they fell back into their pagan ways. Now, with Christ's death, is the time of God's favor when he will reconcile man to himself. The Corinthians must make use of the present opportunity.

Matthew 6, 1-6, 16-18

In the Sermon on the Mount (5, 1-7, 29) Matthew presents Jesus as the new Moses proclaiming the new revelation, what is required of those who would enter the kingdom. In 5, 17-48, Matthew shows the nature of the good works a Christian must perform while in 6, 1-18, he is concerned with the manner in which they should be done. First, the basic principle is laid down (6, 1). What is condemned is not the acting in public, but acting in order to be seen so as to receive the approval of men. Three examples are then given: almsgiving, prayer, and fasting. Each of the illustrations follows the same structure. When one gives alms, prays, or fasts, he is not to advertise it so as to be praised by others. One has already obtained what one seeks and one will obtain no reward from the Father. Rather, the Christian must do his good work in such a way as to bring glory to God and not to himself. Then one will receive a reward from the Father.

Reflection

When Joel spoke the prophecy we heard in the first reading, the people were suffering from a great plague of locusts which were destroying their crops. The prophet saw the plague not only as a punishment for sin but also as a warning that God would come one day in judgment. He therefore called the people to repentance—*all* the people without exceptions, the old, the young, the newly married, and even the priests.

Centuries later St. Paul, in writing to his converts at Corinth, proclaimed the same message of a need for repentance. In his message there was a sense of urgency: "Now is the acceptable time! Now is the day of salvation!"

On this Ash Wednesday the Church once again calls us to repentance by means of the ceremony of the ashes. This call is meant for all of us without exceptions, for the ashes remind us, first, of our human weakness. No matter who we may be, no matter how good we may think we are, because of our weakness we have been guilty of sin and need repentance. The ashes also remind us of the coming judgment of God, for the ashes are a symbol of the inevitability of death when we must face God to give an accounting of our lives. Finally there is a sense of urgency about this call to repentance because we have no idea of when death will claim us.

Repentance means a turning away from sin and a turning toward God, a real change of heart necessary for all of us. Daily Mass during Lent is an excellent way to achieve true repentance. In the lessons you will hear what God's will is for you, that is, just what you are to do to practice repentance. In the Mass you look to God to receive the grace you need to follow out what you learn in the lessons. This Lent is the acceptable time, the time of salvation. We do not know whether we will have another.

Alternate Reflection

Lent, which begins today, is a time of preparation. It looks forward to our annual commemoration of the paschal mystery of Christ at Easter wherein we celebrate his victory over sin and death.

Today in the ceremony of the ashes the Church insists that we face the awesome reality of death: "Remember man that you are dust and unto dust you shall return." A fascinating aspect of death is that it is both certain and uncertain. It is certain in the sense that we know we will one day die. Our ancestors died before us. There were people sitting in church at this time last year who are not here today for one reason: they are dead. And yet this death which is so certain in itself is most uncertain as to time, place, and circumstances. We simply do not know when, where, or how we will die. Most important of all is the question of whether death will find us worthy to share in the victory which Jesus won over sin and death itself—will our death lead to resurrection with Jesus?

Death is also final. None of us can expect to be given a second chance. God has given us an allotted time in which to work out our salvation. It is up to us to use our time well.

One moment wasted by infidelity to God can never be recaptured. We may work harder after a failure, but the one moment lost has passed into eternity, never to return. Nor can we depend on some kind of death bed conversion. On the other hand, if we have really tried to be faithful to God throughout life we need not fear that at the moment of death we will make a sudden reversal and abandon God. It is the present that counts; we cannot change the past nor can we predict the future.

The liturgy has given a sober and awesome reminder: "You are dust and unto dust you shall return." The way in which we live now will determine our future after death. As we live, so shall we die, and as we die, so shall we be for all eternity.

THURSDAY AFTER ASH WEDNESDAY

Deuteronomy 30, 15-20

These verses form part of a final appeal to the people to keep the Law and confront them with the necessity of committing themselves to the covenant. The choice given them is quite simple: life or death, blessings or curse. If they love Yahweh, are loyal to him, and conform their lives to his will they will receive life and many blessings. But if they are disloyal and turn from him to other gods they shall die for they shall be cursed by God. No middle course is allowed.

Luke 9, 22-25

Jesus defines for his disciples, who have just confessed that he is the Messiah (9, 18-20), the nature of his messiahship: he must suffer, die and rise on the third day. This is the divine plan. Jesus then draws out the consequences of discipleship in the light of his own mission. To "take up the cross" was originally meant by Jesus to be taken literally. Those who follow him must be ready to go as far as martyrdom for his sake. Luke, by adding "daily," has adapted this saying to show that following Jesus must be a continual denial of one's self-centered life for the sake of Jesus. It is only by a continual denial of one's self-centered life here on earth that one will gain eternal life. And if man loses the eternal life what has he really profited even though he gains the whole world?

Reflection

Today we are presented with the great issues of life and death—not only this temporal life, but also the eternal life of happiness in heaven; not only death as we know it, but also the unending death of damnation. In the gospel Jesus tells us that he himself must first suffer and endure physical death before entering into eternal life through his resurrection. It is a proclamation of his paschal mystery.

The paschal mystery, put as simply as possible, means that in God's plan Jesus passed through suffering to joy, through humiliation to glory, and through death to life. God's plan for us is that we should share in this same great mystery.

Our first contact with the paschal mystery was our baptism. We then went through a form of death with Christ, a death to sin. And through that death we rose with Christ to share in his life of grace. That was the beginning of our Christian vocation. But all through our lives we share in the paschal mystery in different ways. The Mass is that mystery, for in the Mass Jesus makes present once again the reality of his death and resurrection so that we may share in it. All of our Lenten penance is a sharing in this mystery, as is the suffering that comes to us, be it physical, mental, or emotional. Throughout Lent we look forward to a full liturgical participation in the paschal mystery during Holy Week and Easter.

Moses in the first lesson tells the people that if they are

faithful and loyal to God, they will receive life and many blessings. Jesus is more explicit in the gospel. He warns that faithfulness and loyalty as his disciples means taking up the cross of suffering daily. But he promises us, not merely a temporal blessing, but a sharing in his own eternal life in heaven.

Alternate Reflection

In the days of the reformation in England a bishop refused to recognize the validity of the divorce of King Henry from Catherine of Aragon. There was a principle involved concerning not only the teaching of the Church on marriage and divorce but also the authority of the Pope. It was a principle, and a matter of conscience, for which the bishop was willing to die. As a matter of fact, for his refusal he was condemned to death. It is related that while he was in prison some of his friends came to his cell to plead with him to reconsider in order to save his life. He told his friends that he would give in to their request if they could answer satisfactorily but one question which he would put to them at the end of one week.

During the week the men tried to settle on answers to the questions they thought he would ask about marriage and divorce and papal authority. At the end of the week they approached him and indicated that they were ready for his question. The prisoner said that his question was this: "What profit does he show who gains the whole world and destroys himself in the process?" To this question, originally posed by Jesus himself, the men could offer no answer. Sadly they walked away as the bishop gladly went to his death. As a follower of Christ he had accepted the truth of his words, "Whoever loses his life for my sake will save it." Today he is known as St. John Fischer.

Whatever our temptations may be to abandon Christ, let us pray in the Mass that we will have the courage and the conviction of St. John Fischer, for it will indeed profit us nothing to gain even the whole world if we do not have Jesus to save us from eternal death.

FRIDAY AFTER ASH WEDNESDAY

Isaiah 58, 1-9a

Those who returned from the exile soon began grumbling against the Lord, complaining that though they were correctly keeping the cultic observances, especially the ritual of fasting, they were not receiving what was due them from God: the fulfillment of the divine promises of prosperity and protection from harm. God commands the prophet to tell the "people their wickedness." The accusation is that their fasting is merely an external rite. For on a fast day they continue to pursue their business, make their employees work, and the fast day is even an occasion for quarrelling and acts of violence. The fasting that really pleases God is not putting on sackcloth and ashes but the self-denial involved in helping others, especially, the oppressed, hungry, homeless. This will give their cultic fasting meaning and God will be with them and answer their prayers.

Matthew 9, 14-15

Fasting was required by the Law only on the Day of Atonement. But it had become a pious practice among the Jews to fast more often. This fasting was a penitential practice by which one prepared for the coming of the kingdom. But Jesus and his disciples did not follow this practice and he was asked why. The use of the figure of the marriage feast to describe the messianic age was common. The point of his reply then, as it stands in Matthew, is that the messianic age has arrived with his coming and this is a time for joy not fasting. The reason for the fasting of the Pharisees has been removed since the kingdom is already present. The second half of the verse is a creation of the primitive Church to justify their own fasting. It contains a reference

to Christ's death and points out that there can be a fasting
proper to a Christian which finds its motivation in the Christian
mystery of the Cross.

Reflection

In recent times there has been a new emphasis about
Lent. The fact, however, that we are obliged to fast only
on Ash Wednesday and Good Friday does not mean less
self-denial. What is asked of us now is greater self-denial
in the form of unselfish love and service of others in the
manner described in the first lesson today.

God tells us through this lesson that we are to share our
bread with the hungry, to shelter the oppressed and the
homeless, and not to turn our backs on anyone. To be concerned about others, to be aware of their needs—that takes
real self-denial. If we are concerned only with our own
convenience, our own comfort, our own rights, or even our
own perfection, we will never follow the teaching of our
Lord. His teaching requires that we go out of ourselves to
love and care for others, and that is our Lord's point in
today's gospel about fasting.

In the law of the Old Testament fasting was required
only on the Day of Atonement, but it had become a pious
practice among the Jews to fast more often. Jesus did not
condemn fasting as such. He pointed out that the messianic
era had arrived, that like a bridegroom he would draw his
spouse, the people of God, into an intimate relationship of
love. His great love for us requires that we love one another,
and our love must be like his own; unselfish and self-sacri-
ficing. That is the kind of fasting he wishes.

Alternate Reflection

When some objected to Jesus that his disciples did not fast, he said that for them to fast while he was still with them would make as much sense as mourning at a wedding banquet in the presence of the groom. He said that the time for fasting would come when he would be taken away.

Where does that leave us? Is Jesus still with us so that we should not fast, or has he been taken away so that we should fast? The most obvious answer is that Jesus is not with us; he has been taken away into heaven. In a sense that is correct, and so fasting is in order. But fasting has been de-emphasized in the modern Church partly because of the realization that Jesus is indeed still with us, not only in the Eucharist, but in ourselves as members of his Church through baptism. Jesus has entered into a union of deep love with us, not unlike the marriage union as scripture attests. Because of this union of love our lives should be characterized by a spirit, not of mourning, but of joyful and generous love which overflows to others.

Maybe you know a couple, obviously in love, whose home is always open to anyone. Their mutual love is so great that they seem to have a lot of love left over to share with others. Not only do the parents and the children have many friends, but the whole family without fail is ready and eager to help other people.

We as members of the Church must try to realize that the love Christ has given us must overflow, for we are indeed the family of God. That is why in the first lesson God tells us that what he wants of us is sharing our bread with the hungry, sheltering the oppressed and the homeless, and not turning our backs on anyone. Yes, Jesus is still with us, and he wants his love to spread from our hearts and through our hands.

SATURDAY AFTER ASH WEDNESDAY

Isaiah 58, 9b-14
    The prophet continues with those things which really please the Lord. First, he points out that if the people cease from all kinds of oppression of their neighbor and try rather to help them then they will be blessed by God with happiness, his guidance, and a new strength and vitality. This interior renewal of the individual will be matched outwardly by the restoration of the walls and ruins of Jerusalem. Second, the prophet points out that if they keep the Sabbath holy, refraining from work on that day and seeking only the good of the Lord, completely dedicating the day to him, then God will grant them a divine joy and peace. He will lift them high above all depression and obstacles, and he will also grant them undisturbed possession of the land.

Luke 5, 27-32
    Considering the large banquet he was able to give, Levi's income was probably quite large. Yet at the call of Jesus "leaving everything behind, Levi stood up and became his follower." The verbs here are aorist participles and indicate a continual action. The true disciple is one who is always ready to leave everything to follow the Lord. The Pharisees and their scribes were shocked to see Jesus eating with those who legally were unclean, not keeping the Law as they. The reply of Jesus is ironic. He has not come to call those who already claim to be righteous. For them his call can do nothing because of their self-righteousness. But for those who are ready to admit their sinfulness his call will lead to repentance.

Reflection

    Suppose you are not feeling very well. You go to your doctor and after a thorough examination he tells you that you have a severe case of diabetes. You must go on a very strict diet. You have to give up most of your favorite foods, and drinking is out of the question. The doctor warns you that it is a matter of life or death. I think you would go along with what the doctor says. You would indeed be very foolish to ignore his diagnosis and pretend that you are not sick at all. The best doctor in the world would be of absolutely no help to you unless you were first willing to admit that you were sick, that you needed his services.

The Pharisees and the scribes in today's gospel were very foolish people. They were self-righteous, that is, right in their own eyes but not in the eyes of God. When Jesus said, "The healthy do not need a physician," he was being ironic, meaning the opposite of what he said in the sense that the Pharisees and the scribes were not healthy at all. They were seriously sick with the spiritual disease of selfishness and pride. They needed to go on a spiritual diet like the one prescribed in the first lesson today: they needed to give up following their own ways and seeking their own interests. But even Jesus could not help them because they were unwilling to admit that they were sick.

Jesus is our spiritual physician. He has the skill and the means to cure us of sin if we only follow his advice and his directions. First we must be humble and honest enough to accept his diagnosis. Today before communion we will admit to Jesus that we are spiritually ill and that we need his help. We will say, "Lord, I am not worthy to receive you, but only say the word and I shall be healed." That humble admission is the first step on the road to a full recovery from the sickness of sin.

Alternate Reflection

When Levi, whose other name was Matthew, was called by Jesus to be an apostle, his occupation was that of a tax collector, usually a lucrative position in those days. In view of the great reception he was able to give in his own home for Jesus, he was apparently a wealthy man. St. Luke notes that when he was called, Levi left everything for Jesus. Considering his wealth, his decision to follow Jesus involved a greater sacrifice than that of the apostles called earlier, who were fisherman. It was a point missed by the Pharisees.

When the Pharisees objected to Jesus' association with men like Levi, an undesirable in their eyes, and others who did not keep the Law according to their interpretation, he answered that he had come to call sinners. When Jesus used the term, sinners, he did not intend that it should be understood according to the mind of the Pharisees. Actually it was his way of saying that he had come to call everyone, since all men in one way or another are sinners. Even the Pharisees would have been called, except that they precluded themselves by their self-righteousness, by their judgment that they were better than anybody else, and by their blind decision that they did not need Jesus.

Today the Church of Jesus Christ calls everyone; only those are excluded who have excluded themselves. It is indeed a sad, scandalous situation when the members of any parish refuse to welcome someone warmly into their number, whether it be because of his low economic or social status or because of his poor reputation. It is your business to make everyone feel welcome in church, no matter how he may be dressed, or how unappealing he may appear, or what others may say of him. The fact that he comes to church must be taken as a sign that he wishes to respond to Jesus, and, who knows, his response may involve an even greater sacrifice than that of Levi. To wish to exclude anyone is to be guilty of the self-righteousness of the Pharisees, who alone deserved to be excluded.

MONDAY OF THE FIRST WEEK

Leviticus 19, 1-2, 11-18

The unifying characteristic of the Holiness Code (Lv 17-26) is that God is holy, i.e., "wholly other," separated from all that is profane. Israel, through its election by God and his active presence, has also become holy. This holiness is maintained by cultic ritual and by a life lived in accordance with the moral will of God. The emphasis in this passage is on the need to practice justice and charity in one's social dealings. One is to avoid various kinds of underhand dealings with his companions (11-12); the economically or physically stronger person is not to use his advantage over weaker and helpless people (13-14); court proceedings are to be marked by strict adherence to justice (15-16). Also feelings of hatred and vengeance are to be uprooted from one's heart and one should correct his brother (17). Finally, all is summed up in the command to love one's neighbor as oneself. Here, neighbor refers to a fellow Israelite.

Matthew 25, 31-46

This passage concludes the last discourse of Jesus in Matthew's gospel. It is intended as the final word of Jesus to his disciples in which he sets forth the core of his moral teaching. The scene pictured is the second coming of Christ at the end of time when all the nations have been gathered before him for judgment. Jesus is called King, a divine title. The basis upon which men are judged is their behavior toward their fellow man, their love for their neighbor as expressed in deeds. Jesus identifies himself with those to whom service is given or refused so that when one serves his fellow man in love, or refuses this service, he is serving Jesus or refusing to serve Jesus. It sur-

prised both the blessed and the condemned that they have
encountered Jesus, and hence God, in their fellow man. They
thought that there was a distinction between serving God and
their fellow man.

Reflection

It must have been a wonderful thing to have lived with
Jesus when he was on this earth. What a great privilege it
was for Peter, James, and John to have known our Lord personally and intimately. We naturally wish that we could
have lived with Jesus, and I think we feel that we would
have been completely devoted to him.

As a matter of fact many people who lived with Jesus
either did not recognize him or failed to respond to him.
And today it may be that we ourselves sometimes do not
recognize Jesus or fail to respond to him. We do not have
to wish that we could have lived at the time of our Lord.
The truth is that he is living among us right now. He is
present in this world not only in the Eucharist but also in
the people with whom we live. He is all around us.

In today's gospel Jesus tells us that what we do to one
of his brothers we do to him. Notice that he does not say
that it is *as if* we do it to him, or that he will *consider* what
we do to others as done to himself. We must not water
down the truth. Jesus lives in others. What we do to them,
we do to Jesus.

In the first reading today we heard many practical direc-
tives for dealing with people, all of which are summed up
in the one command, "You shall love your neighbor as yourself." Among the Old Testament people the word "neighbor"
was understood as referring to a fellow Israelite. Jesus gave
this commandment two new dimensions. First, neighbor in-

cludes everyone. Secondly, Jesus lives in our fellow human
beings, our neighbors.

There is no sense in daydreaming about how much we
love Jesus or in imagining all the great things we would
like to do for him. We are right in seeking him here in the
Eucharist, but still more is needed. He is all around us in
the people we live with and meet every day. When our time
for judgment comes, Jesus will want to know whether we
have loved him, not only by our worship of him in the
liturgy, but also by finding him and serving him in our
fellow human beings.

Alternate Reflection

When St. Martin of Tours was but a catechumen and a
soldier in the army, a poor man approached him and asked
for an alms. Martin had no money, but seeing the man shiv-
ering in the cold he took his cloak from his shoulders, cut
it in two with his sword, and gave half to the beggar. Later
that night Martin was rewarded with a vision of Jesus wear-
ing the half of the cloak he had given away.

Upon hearing this story, some people immediately think
that Jesus had come down from heaven and disguised himself as the beggar. Such was not the case, as we learn in
today's gospel. Jesus said quite plainly, and his words must
be taken as they stand, "I assure you, as often as you did
it for one of my least brothers, you did it for me." Jesus is
present and living in others, those whom we are privileged
to serve in love. This great truth has been understood by
the saints, and has motivated their manner of acting.

St. Vincent de Paul, for example, made meditation and
prayer a very important part of his life. Despite the great
value he placed on them, whenever someone needed him he

quickly and cheerfully left the chapel to be of service. When a priest of his congregation once asked him if it were not more important to remain at prayer, Vincent replied, "I am leaving God for God." He understood the lesson taught by our Lord in today's gospel.

We do well in praying to God at Mass, and this is necessary. At the end of Mass you hear these words, "Go in peace to love and serve the Lord." Indeed, we will fulfill these words if we go forth to serve others for the love of God.

TUESDAY OF THE FIRST WEEK

Isaiah 55, 10-11

The context of these two verses is the conclusion to Deutero-Isaiah in which Israel is invited to turn to God and have faith in him and he will give them salvation. In vv. 8 and 9 reference is made to the difficulty of understanding God's way of salvation. One is to acknowledge God's saving purpose but no one should think he knows all that is involved in this salvation. The ways of God are not the ways of man. Then we have these two verses. The point is that if God has spoken and promised salvation, it will come, for God's word is always effective; what it proclaims will be fulfilled. But the author does not mean to say that the word of God works automatically, in a magical way. If it is to be effective in a man, the man must accept it. But the acceptance itself also comes from God.

Matthew 6, 7-15

While speaking of the proper way to pray (5-6) Jesus tells his disciples that their prayers must not be like those of the Gentiles. The Father already knows their needs and he does not need a cataloguing of them. Christ then presents the model way to pray. The **Lord's Prayer** is not concerned with particular petitions but is completely directed to something more important: the eschatological realization of the kingdom. The first three petitions ask that this be soon. The fourth petition repeats the same idea since what it asks for is "the bread for tomorrow," i.e., the eschato-logical banquet. This is followed by a petition for forgiveness at the Judgment and a plea for God to protect one from apostasy, from falling into the clutches of evil (the evil one?), at the time of the great eschatological test. Verses 14 and 15 are a commentary on the fifth petition and stress the necessity of forgiveness of others to receive forgiveness from God.

Reflection

The power of speech, or communication, is one of the most wonderful gifts that God has given us. Through words we can tell others our thoughts, our feelings, our hopes, and our joys. What we say to others in words can change completely their attitude toward us and establish a new relationship.

God's word is found in the sacred scriptures, a word that we hear every day in Mass. Through his word God tells us of himself, his thoughts, and his wishes for us. Through his word he wants to establish a special relationship with us, one of love. And this word of God has real power to accomplish a change in us. As we just heard in today's lesson, God says, "My word shall not return to me void, but shall do my will, achieving the end for which I sent it." The word of God, however, will not produce its effect without our cooperation. We must try to listen to God's word actively and attentively, especially at Mass. Here we can learn what God is like, how he feels toward us, and what he expects from us.

And God wants to hear our words too. Words spoken to God are prayer. Simple words are best, words like "I love you—I need you—I'd do anything for you." This simplicity in prayer is what Jesus had in mind when he said, "In your prayers do not rattle on like the pagans." The prayer he taught, the *Our Father,* was intended to be a model for prayer. Jesus did not mean that the words of the *Our Father* are the only ones we should use in prayer. It is the spirit behind those words which counts, a spirit of simplicity, directness, and sincerity.

Words are wonderful, especially the word of God. We must listen to that word with great attention. Our words will be pretty wonderful too if we pray in the way our Savior taught us.

Alternate Reflection

Throughout his life Jesus referred to God as "*my* Father." And of course God, the first person of the Trinity, is the Father of Jesus in a unique sense. The striking thing about Jesus' lesson on how to pray is that he told his disciples and us that we should address his Father in heaven as "*our* Father." Obviously we can never be the child of God in the same way as Jesus, for we would then be God too as Jesus is, but in our own way we really do become God's child through baptism.

A person becomes the child of someone by receiving life from him. In baptism we really do receive a share in the life of God, which we call sanctifying grace. Jesus chose water as the sacred sign of baptism, and a fitting sign it is. Without water the growing things of the earth wither and die. You have experienced this fact if, during the heat of the summer, you have neglected to water your lawn. But with water the plants and the trees and the grass come alive with a vibrant growth. And with the water of baptism we came alive with the vitality of God himself. God from eternity has given his life to his Son, and through his Son in baptism he has given a share in his life to us so that we have become his children.

A good parent does more than pass on life. He enters into a relationship of love with his child. He cares for him and is concerned about him. And that is God's relationship with us through Christ.

To call God "our Father" is no fiction. Rather it reflects a profound truth upon which we should meditate, not only so that we may appreciate God's gift of divine life to us, but also so that our prayer may be in the right spirit. When we pray we speak not only to God who has made the universe and who is the Lord and Master of all creation, but also to God who truly is our Father, and who has love and concern for us as his children.

WEDNESDAY OF THE FIRST WEEK

Jonah 3, 1-10

Jonah had been commanded by Yahweh to preach to the pagan city of Nineveh but he fled from the task. In a storm at sea he was cast into the waters only to be swallowed by a great fish and vomited on the shore. Jonah then received a second call from God to go and preach to Nineveh. This time he obeyed and his message to the city was very brief. Surprisingly, the Ninevites repented and stood in striking contrast to the Israelites who, despite all the preaching of the prophets, remained in their sin. The King even decreed a general fast which was to include everyone in the hope that the Lord would forgive and not destroy the city. God, seeing their repentance, decided not to destroy them. This is what Jonah feared might happen and why he had run away. To him Yahweh was God of the Jews only. But the point of the book is that God is concerned for all men.

Luke 11, 29-32

The people seek a sign from Jesus, some spectacular proof that he is the emissary of God as he claims. But Jesus replies that the only proof of his credentials he will give them is that which Jonah offered to the people of Nineveh. Jonah simply presented them with the word of God, a call to repentance, and they

responded! Jesus presents his generation with the same credentials: the word of God, a call to repentance. But unlike the gen-
tile Ninevites they have not responded to one greater than Jonah.
Being an evil generation they can not recognize the voice of God
when they hear it and will be condemned by the Ninevites at the
Judgment. Also, the Queen of Sheba, who came from afar to seek
Wisdom from Solomon, will condemn them at the Judgment for
they have rejected one who is greater than Solomon, Wisdom in-
carnate.

Reflection

One of the most impressive of all Catholic shrines is that
of Lourdes in France. There miraculous cures have occurred,
many of them authenticated through the most intense scrut-
iny by a team of experts. To see, and even more to experience personally, such a miracle would indeed be a tremendous bolstering of one's faith.

The people in today's gospel were looking for some such
miracle from Jesus, some spectacular proof of his claims. But
Jesus refused to give any extraordinary sign to them. His
preaching of the word of God should have been sign enough.
He pointed out that the people of Nineveh, pagans though
they were, accepted Jonah, and he was much greater than
Jonah.

Though we are people of faith, it is only natural that
once in a while we wish for some extraordinary sign from
God to confirm our faith. For the most part, however, we
must live by and accept the ordinary signs of God's activity
among us, the most important of which are found in
the Mass. First is the sign of our coming together as God's
people. We ourselves are a sign of the presence of Jesus, for
as Jesus promised, "Where two or three are gathered in my
name, there am I in their midst." Actually it is Jesus who continues to pray within us as members of his Body. The word

of God is also a sign. The *Constitution on the Sacred Liturgy* reminds us that Jesus "is present in his word, since it is he himself who speaks when the holy scriptures are read in the Church" (7). It is Jesus who renews the offering of himself in the sacred sign of the consecration, and Jesus who comes to us under the sign of food and drink.

Summing up these ideas, the *Constitution on the Sacred Liturgy* declares, "In the liturgy the sanctification of man is signified by signs perceptible to the senses and is effected in a way which corresponds with each of these signs; in the liturgy the whole public worship is performed by the mystical body of Jesus Christ, that is, by the head and members" (7).

The signs of the Mass are simple, but their spiritual effects are extraordinary, for they are a sign of the presence and activity of one who is much greater than Jonah or anyone else. It is Jesus himself who lives and acts through the sacred signs of the Mass.

Alternate Reflection

Whenever we hear of Jonah, we think of the incident in which he was swallowed by the great fish. Actually that story was but a prelude to today's first lesson about Jonah. God wanted Jonah to preach to the pagan city of Nineveh, but Jonah felt that only Jews should hear the word of God, and so he tried to run away. In a storm at sea, brought on by God's anger, he was cast into the water only to be swallowed by the fish and then vomited on the shore. He received a second command from God to preach to the pagans of Nineveh. This time he obeyed, and much to his surprise the people heeded the word of God and repented. The point of the story is that God cares about *all* men and wills their salvation.

There are times in life when we are tempted to wonder whether God really cares about us or even has time for little people like us. Is he too busy running the universe, too concerned about the big important people who are responsible for the major events which shape history itself? God does care and has great concern, because he has sent someone to us who is even greater than Jonah. In the Mass we hear the words of Jesus. In the Mass we pray to God through, with, and in Jesus. In the Mass God gives us the gift of his Son in holy communion.

God showed his care and love for the people of Nineveh by sending Jonah to them. His love and concern for us are greater in the degree in which Jesus is greater than Jonah.

THURSDAY OF THE FIRST WEEK

Esther 14, 1, 3-5, 12-14 (C, 12, 14-16, 23-15)

The book of Esther tells of the plot of Haman, the minister of King Xerxes of Persia, to destroy in a single day all the Jews living in the Persian Empire. Meanwhile, Esther, a Jew, is chosen queen and she prevents the destruction of her people by appealing to the King. This passage contains her prayer before she approaches the King to seek his intervention. She is frightened because it is a law of Persia that anyone "who goes to the King in the inner court without being summoned, suffers the automatic penalty of death" (4, 11), unless the King spares the person's life. But despite this possibility of death she is ready to take the risk for her people and so she puts her trust in the Lord and asks him for courage for herself, the success of her mission, and the destruction of the enemies of her people.

Matthew 7, 7-12

In 6, 33, Christ tells his disciples to seek first the kingdom and all other things will be given as well (see Mt 6, 7-15). Here, the conscious repetition of the same theme, ask-receive, seek-find, knock-be-opened, is to emphasize to the disciples that God does hear their prayers and answers them and to encourage them in presenting their petitions to God. The reason they can have confidence that God hears their prayers and answers them is that God is their heavenly Father. Evil men give good gifts to their children who ask for them; **a fortiori** God, who is good, will certainly give the kingdom, and all that is needed to attain it, to those who ask. Verse 12 is a statement of the Golden Rule and is meant to be a summation of all that has gone before in the Sermon on the Mount. One must follow it if one wishes one's petition to be heard.

Reflection

Imagine this scene which takes place somewhere every day. A person surrounded by his family lies dying in a hospital bed. The doctors have admitted that the case is medically hopeless. A member of the family quietly says, "I guess all we can do now is pray." All we can do now is pray. . . . Such a statement betrays an attitude that prayer is but a last resort in dire circumstances.

How different was the attitude and teaching of Jesus about prayer. His words to us today indicate that prayer must be an habitual part of our life in all of its circumstances. A little child does not turn to his parents only when he is in serious trouble. He is completely dependent on them and somehow knows that all good things come from them. He looks to his parents for food when he is hungry, he runs to them for comfort when he has skinned his knee or had his feelings hurt, he seeks solace from them when he is lonely and blue. Above all he wants to feel that he belongs, that he has their love and interest all the time.

No matter how young or old we may be, in relation to God we are like little children, and God is a Father more loving and interested than even the best of human parents. He wants us to look to him in all the circumstances of our lives, not merely when we are in serious trouble. It is true that the prayer of Esther in today's first reading was a plea when her life was in danger. She was about to intervene with King Xerxes to thwart a plot to destroy her fellow Jews, even though the law of Persia stated that anyone who approached the King in his inner court without being summoned would suffer the penalty of automatic death. Esther's prayer in her moment of supreme danger was prompted by her habitual practice of turning to God for help. She was not praying because there was nothing else she could think of. Her words show that she understood not only God's concern and power, but also her complete dependence on him: "You alone are God. Help me, who am alone and have no help but you." It was the prayer of a little child before God her Father.

Prayer, then, is not some last ditch effort to ward off impending disaster as suggested in the words heard so often, "All we can do now is pray." It should instead be a child's confident turning to God as a loving Father in all the circumstances of our lives.

Alternate Reflection

The words of our Lord, "Ask and you will receive," indicate that God does answer our prayers. Our Lord's insistence on this fact puts one in mind of the well-known story of the little girl who was taunted by her friends that God had not answered her prayer because she did not receive something she had prayed for. The little girl responded, "God answered my prayer; it's just that his answer was 'No.' "

The truth of the matter is that God does not have to be

informed as to what our needs are. He knows them better than we, and actually grants what we really need, though not always what we think we need. St. Augustine put it succinctly when he said, "If our prayers seem not answered, it is because either we do not ask rightly or we do not ask for the right thing."

God, more than the best of parents, is concerned with giving us the right thing, but he does will that his gifts come to us in answer to our prayers. Every parent should be able to understand why God wants us to ask for things. Good parents will take care of their children, but they are pleased when their children turn to them with confidence, as well as politeness, for they thereby show that they recognize both the ability of their parents to help as well as their love which will move them to help.

All prayer should be worship of God, that is, a recognition of God's power and love, even the prayer of petition. When we pray to God with humility, realizing his almighty power, and with confidence, recognizing his love, he will give us the good things we need.

FRIDAY OF THE FIRST WEEK

Ezekiel 18, 21-28

Among the exiles the prevalent view was that their suffering was to be explained by the doctrine of corporate guilt: they were being punished for the sins of their fathers. Their attitude was one of despair and fatalism and indirectly they were excusing themselves from any sin. To them God was acting unfairly in their regard. In ch. 18 Ezekiel flatly tells them that each man is accountable to God only for his own actions. In vv. 21-28 Ezekiel goes on to point out that if the wicked man truly repents and orders his life according to God's will, he will be forgiven and be blessed by God; he will be given life. All of his wickedness will be forgotten because of his personal decision for God. But if the virtuous man turns from God, by a personal decision on his part, and does evil, he will die and his good deeds will count for nothing. It is not that God is unfair but that the injustice is on the part of those who reject God.

Matthew 5, 20-26

This is the first of six illustrations which explain the general principle on the nature of good works found in 5, 17-19 (see Wednesday of the third week). The general principle states that God desires not the mere external observance of the letter of the Law but the observance of the spirit of the Law found in the law of love. This is the righteousness that exceeds that of the scribes and Pharisees. The letter of the Law forbids killing, but the spirit of the Law forbids the anger that motivates it and the expression of this anger in speech. They are as bad as murder itself and deserve the same punishment. In the two sayings that follow the emphasis is on the urgency of reconciliation (23-26). The duty of reconciliation with one's brother has primacy even over cultic duties. The case envisioned here is one in which a person has aroused anger in another. The time for reconciliation is now, for the judgment is coming when it will be too late.

Reflection

A high school boy was very eager to play with his school's football team. His father was delighted with the idea, but he warned his son that he had to keep up his studies. He told him that if his marks went down after the first year of football, he would not be allowed to play the following year. All the while the father was hoping that the boy would continue to do well in his classes because he did not want to punish his son by not letting him play football.

Almost all parents have had the feeling that discipline of children is harder on them than it is on the children, but they know that it is something they must do. God as our Father definitely takes no delight in punishing us for our sins, but it is something that he does in justice. The words of the first lesson reveal God's attitude, "Do I indeed derive any pleasure from the death of the wicked? says the Lord. Do I not rather rejoice when he turns from his evil way that he may live?"

On the other hand, God does not lower the standards required of us; he demands that we keep our grades up. That is what Jesus is talking about in today's gospel. He points out that mere external observance of the letter of the Law (getting by with D's) is not good enough. It is the observance of the spirit of the Law found in the supreme law of love (getting straight A's) that really counts, and it is this holiness, which surpasses that of the scribes and the Pharisees, which will win entrance for us into the kingdom of God.

Though God demands much of us, he is in a sense pulling for us all the time. We must remember that God is a loving Father who wants to punish us even less than we want to be punished.

Alternate Reflection

Sometime or other you have heard someone say something like "Any friend of Fred is a friend of mine." The expression of course means that the person has a high regard and esteem for Fred. And out of consideration for Fred, he would want to favor, and never offend, any friend of his.

Jesus had the same principle in mind when he said that we should first be reconciled with anyone we have offended before offering our gift at the altar. Any friend of God should be a friend of ours, or to put it more correctly, we should love and respect any child of God. To fail to do so is to fail to love and respect God. God says, as would any good parent, "Love me, love my children."

We go to Mass to worship God by giving him a Gift in sacrifice. If we have enmity in our heart for anyone, God prefers that we leave the Gift and first become reconciled with the one we have offended. Otherwise our Gift giving is meaningless; it is the mere external observance of religion practiced by the Pharisees and resoundingly condemned by Jesus.

I suppose that it would be pretty dramatic if we all were to stop Mass, leave church, and seek out anyone we have wilfully hurt. The very least we can do, however, is pray to God now for forgiveness, and, before we return to Mass, go to anyone we have offended and offer our apologies. Our next Mass then will have much more meaning and be much more pleasing to God.

SATURDAY OF THE FIRST WEEK

Deuteronomy 26, 16-19

These verses are a concluding exhortation after the promulgation of the Law (chs. 5-26). Since the book is addressed to a generation of Israelites who lived long after the actual Sinai event, the "this day" is the liturgical **now.** The present generation, to whom the Law has just been read in a liturgical rite, is now asked to renew the covenant with Yahweh. Moses is presented as a mediator between Yahweh and the people in the making of the covenant. The Lord has revealed the Law to them and has promised to cherish and bless them in a most special way if they will but obey him. The people have heard the Law and they declare that they are ready to keep it. Thus each generation renews the covenant for itself.

Matthew 5, 43-48

This is the sixth illustration of the principle that Matthew presents on the nature of good works (see Wednesday of third week). The precept of love of neighbor is quoted from Lv 19, 18. The command to hate one's enemies is not found in the Old Testament. But since the Jews, for the most part, limited the interpretation of the word "neighbor" to a fellow Israelite this might be the expression of a popular understanding of the love of one's neighbor. In the context "enemies" probably refers to the persecutors of the early Church. The point is that the spirit of the Law, the law of love, demands that the Christian's love be indescriminate just as the Father is indescriminate in his distribution of the sun and rain. The Christian's love must be universal and not just for members of his own group, which is a natural thing. But such a universal and disinterested love one will be perfect as the Father is perfect.

Reflection

The covenant of Sinai was mediated by Moses and sealed in the blood of animal sacrifice. It was an agreement whereby God would be the God of the Israelites and they would be his people, provided they kept his commandments. The new covenant was mediated by Jesus Christ and sealed in his own blood on the cross. We by our baptism are the new people of God, the people of this new covenant, and we too are called upon to keep his commandments.

The blood of Christ is not only the seal of the new covenant, but also a special sign of the love of God for us, his people, as well as a sign of how great our love must be. In today's gospel Jesus emphasizes our love for our fellow human beings. It is to be a love like his own. When Jesus says that we must love even our enemies and pray for our persecutors, he is teaching a commandment he himself followed. From the cross he prayed for his persecutors and he died on the cross out of love for those who were his enemies by sin.

Christianity is a joyful, happy religion, but this does not mean that those whom we are commanded to love are limited to pleasant, agreeable people. True joy and real happiness come from being like Jesus, and Jesus excluded no one from his love, neither his big enemies or his little ones—neither the people who put him to death nor those who merely nagged him and bothered him when he needed peace and quiet.

The people addressed in today's first lesson lived long after the actual sealing of the old covenant. These words were proclaimed to them in a liturgical rite so that they might personally renew for themselves the covenant with God. When we come to the end of Lent on Holy Saturday, we will be invited in a liturgical rite to renew our covenant with God through the renewal of our baptism. That renewal will mean little unless during Lent we have made even greater efforts to practice the great commandment of love, a love like that of Jesus which excluded no one.

Alternate Reflection

Today's first lesson was addressed to a generation of Israelites who lived long after the covenant of Sinai when God promised that the people would be peculiarly his own, provided they kept his commandments. The people to whom this passage was read in a liturgical rite were asked to renew the covenant with God by their own personal commitment to him.

The new covenant was sealed in the blood of Jesus, and we entered into that covenant through our baptism. It has been traditional in the Church that the season of Lent be dedicated in a special way to this sacrament. At the end of Lent we will be asked to renew our baptism in a formal manner during the Holy Saturday liturgy. That will be a very important liturgical rite, but we certainly do not have to wait until Holy Saturday to make a personal renewal of our baptism, our covenant with God, the pledge of our complete devotion to him. After all, married couples do not have to wait until the anniversary of their wedding to renew their marriage vows; it is something they should do every day as they express their love for each other. And so the renewal of our baptism is something we can do today within Mass.

During the Eucharistic Prayer the bread will become the body of Christ and the wine will become his blood, "the blood of the new and everlasting covenant." Thereby our Lord will re-present the sacrificial offering of himself to his Father, the expression of his complete dedication to the Father, his absolute fidelity, and his total love. He invites us today to join with him in this sacrifice. Let us say within ourselves, "Father, with Christ we make the complete gift of ourselves to you." And that will be a true renewal of our baptism, our covenant with God.

MONDAY OF THE SECOND WEEK

Daniel 9, 4b-10

This is part of the prayer Daniel is reported to have said when trying to come to an understanding of Jeremiah's prophecy that the term of the desolation of Jerusalem was to be only 70 years. The prayer may be a later addition to the text for it is a prayer of the community in which the community acknowledges its guilt and asks for the restoration of Jerusalem. In the section used for today's reading Israel first confesses that she has sinned, that she has been unfaithful to the covenant, disobeying God and the prophets who spoke in his name (4-6). Therefore, God is completely just in continuing to punish his people and Israel is shamefaced before him (7-8). Finally, she appeals to his mercy and asks forgiveness (9-10).

Luke 6, 36-38

>   Part of Luke's "Great Discourse" (6, 17-49). Characteristic
> of life in the kingdom of God is love of neighbor, a generous and
> active interest in the true welfare of others which is at the same
> time disinterested and universal, not deterred by hatred or
> abuse or the seeking of a return (6, 32-35). If one acts in this
> way he is being merciful as the Father is merciful and he is a
> true son of the Most High (36). Such a love is also generous in
> forgiving and does not condemn others. The more generous a
> man is in this regard, all the more will God pour out on him
> His gifts of mercy and forgiveness.

Reflection

There are several lessons our Lord seemed never to tire
of repeating. His favorite was the lesson of love, and one
aspect of love that he insisted on was that of forgiveness.
Perhaps he persevered in his teaching about forgiveness
because he realized how difficult a virtue it is for us. How
often have you heard someone say, "I forgive, but I just
can't forget"? Maybe you have said it yourself. That attitude
—forgiving but not forgetting—is in reality far from the ideal
that our Lord had in mind. To nurse hurt feelings, while
mouthing words of pardon, is not really Christian forgiveness at all. "I just don't want to get burned again," we say,
and what we actually mean is that we now wish to alter our
relationship with the person who has offended us.

Jesus wants us to practice his kind of forgiveness. After
an injury, for which a person is sorry, nothing changes. Remember what Peter did to Jesus at the time of his passion.
Not once, but three times he denied that he even knew Jesus.
Before that denial Jesus had promised Peter that he would
be the head of the Church, and despite Peter's denials Jesus
stuck to his promise. Jesus didn't say, "Well, Peter, I forgive
you, but I just can't forget your disloyalty and so someone

else will have to take your place." Even Judas could have been restored to his position as an apostle if he had not despaired.

We ourselves hope for forgiveness from God, real forgiveness. We pray that God will completely forget our sins and keep us in his loving care. Jesus warns, however, that we will enjoy such total forgiveness from God only if we have learned to practice it ourselves. True forgiveness involves a kind of spiritual amnesia, and it is a real part of the love that Jesus both taught and practiced.

Alternate Reflection

There are three words which most of us find very difficult to say and mean. Those three words are, "I was wrong." Simple words they are, but even in little matters they are hard to say. If we knock over a glass and break it, it is the fault of someone who left it where they should not have. If we are late for an appointment, it is the fault of the alarm clock which failed to go off. And even when we have sinned, it is hard to admit our fault; we look for excuses.

The prayer recorded in the first reading is refreshing in that it is an honest admission of guilt. In the prayer the people acknowledge that they have sinned, that they have been unfaithful to the covenant and disobeyed God and his messengers. In effect they say, "We were wrong," those words so difficult to say and mean.

There are three other words equally difficult to say and mean, and those words are, "I am sorry." They are words which should follow "I was wrong." Have we been wrong? If we have our ideals set as high as Jesus requires in today's gospel, maybe we can see how wrong we are. Are we as compassionate as God is? If not, then we are wrong. Are we as forgiving as God is? If not, then we are wrong. Are we as generous in giving as God is? If not, then we are wrong.

If we are wrong, we must bring ourselves to say, and to mean, "I am sorry." The sincerity of those three little words will be measured by our effort to match the ideal of goodness and love which Jesus has taught us by word and example.

TUESDAY OF THE SECOND WEEK

Isaiah 1, 10, 16-20

The theme of 1, 10-20, is that sacrifice without morality is worthless. The rulers and people of Jerusalem are addressed as the "princes of Sodom" and "people of Gomorrah." These two cities are presented as symbols of moral perversion, examples of the immorality of the people and rulers of Jerusalem. In 11-15 Yahweh condemns their sacrifices and says that they are loathsome to him for all he sees is their hands full of blood. Before these sacrifices are acceptable to him they must purify themselves, not with some ritual purification but by putting aside every evil action and doing good. This doing good is described above all in terms of duties towards the neighbor, represented by the orphan and the widow (16-17). Finally, he reminds them that if they sincerely repent and turn to him in obedience even the most serious sins can be forgiven and they shall be saved; but if they refuse they will be destroyed.

Matthew 23, 1-12

Chapter 23 is a summary of Jesus' charges against the scribes and Pharisees. To understand the chapter properly one has to keep in mind that the Church of Matthew was still deeply involved in controversy with the Jews. The passage is a caricature and a repudiation of certain tendencies that must have been prevalent enough. It is a portrait of unbelief at any time and a warning to the Church. Jesus does not question the authority of the scribes. His main criticism is not aimed at their teaching but at the discrepancy between what they teach and what they do. Jesus accuses them of hypocrisy, lack of charity, vanity, and ostentation. They are not to be imitated. The Christian leader must be humble and the servant of all. All Christians are brothers under God who is the Father of all. The only teacher they are to have is Jesus.

Reflection

A priest once remarked, "It is a shame that I do not practice what I preach, but it would be far worse if I were to preach what I practice." The statement was made in good humor, but as a matter of fact we are not inclined to like people who do not practice what they preach. More seriously, we are not inclined to listen to what they have to say. You can imagine how you would feel if your doctor were to insist that you give up smoking as he blows cigarette smoke in your face.

Sometimes we hear about people who have left the Church because they maintain that bishops and priests do not practice what they preach. Even if their claims were true, such people should remember that our Lord in today's gospel told the people to follow the teaching of their leaders because they had succeeded Moses as teachers, even though they did not follow that teaching themselves. But wait a minute. Who really is the teacher of our faith? Who really is the preacher to whom we must listen? It is Jesus Christ. The pope, the bishops, the priests, only hand on to us the word of Christ.

The real question, then, is what about the example of Christ. He was one who indeed practiced what he preached. He told us to love our enemies, and he redeemed those who by sin were his enemies. He said that we should do good to our persecutors, and he forgave those who put him to death. He proclaimed that no one could have greater love than to lay down his life for a friend, and he died out of love for his Father and us.

The best sermon at any Mass is still the example of Christ, which in the Mass is made present on our altar: the sacrificial offering of himself to his Father.

Alternate Reflection

The background of today's first reading is that God was not pleased with the liturgical sacrifices of his people, for in God's eyes prayer and sacrifice without good living are worthless. This word of God to us today means that we must live our sacrifice of the Mass. Let's think about that a little.

In the Mass we offer ourselves with Jesus to God our Father to express our complete love for him; we make the gift of ourselves through, with, and in Christ. Then to show that he is pleased with our offering, God makes a return gift to us in holy communion. We receive the resurrected, glorified body of Christ and enter into intimate union with him.

When we leave this place of worship we should do so to continue a life of worship. The rest of the day must be a continuation of the offering of ourselves in the Mass. In the holy sacrifice we have said that we wish to give ourselves completely to God; now we must live in accord with that dedication. Throughout the day we must do nothing that we would have to be ashamed to give to God in the next Mass we offer. After all, when we come to Mass we can offer only what we are and what we have done. We must do nothing that would contradict the offering we have already made.

Our communion is a sharing in the resurrection of Christ, his victory over sin. We must then go forth to witness that resurrection by showing in our lives that Christ has conquered sin in us personally.

We must live the Mass.

WEDNESDAY OF THE SECOND WEEK

Jeremiah 18, 18-20

A report of one of several attempts on the prophet's life. Neither the circumstances nor time of this attempt are known but the plot is clear, his enemies will listen carefully to what he says and seek an opportunity for condemning him; they will try to entrap him in his speech. To these schemers Jeremiah's death would be of no importance for the priestly instruction, the prophetical word, and the sapiential counsel would not cease with his death. What hurts Jeremiah is that he has stood before the Lord asking Him to remove His wrath from just these men and they are now repaying this favor with evil.

Matthew 20, 17-28

On his final journey to Jerusalem Jesus predicts his passion for the third time. But it is obvious from the following episode that the Twelve still do not grasp what he is talking about. They still expect some kind of a worldly triumph. Matthew spares the reputation of James and John by having their mother make the request for the two first places in the kingdom. When Jesus asks them if they are ready to share his fate they affirm that they are. Jesus then dismisses the whole question by saying it is the Father who determines such things. Since the indignation of the disciples arises from the same motive that had brought on the request from the sons of Zebedee, Jesus draws a lesson for all from the episode. Whoever has a position of greatness in the Church must be the servant of all. The example is Christ himself who has come to serve others even to the point of giving his life for all men so that all may be saved.

Reflection

The scene in today's gospel is a very natural one, a mother trying to gain a place of honor for her two sons. The context suggests that James and John were not at all hesitant about having their mother intercede for them. Our Lord's reply indicates that Christianity requires a generous service without the thought of reward as a motive. A reward there will be from the Father, and it is a strong incentive, but Jesus asks that we be as unselfish as he was in the service of his fellow men.

It is no easy thing to give of ourselves to others without some kind of recompense, but if we look for that kind of satisfaction I am afraid that we will not be very good disciples of Jesus Christ. If you are a parent, you know that children do not always appreciate what you are trying to do for them and take a lot for granted. Perhaps you have to take care of older parents, and the elderly without realizing it can be very demanding on your time with a considerable taxing of your nerves and your patience. It is especially difficult when the people you are helping manifest no gratitude at all, but the worst possible situation is to have them turn against you completely. Jeremiah the prophet was in just such a situation. Those who were plotting his death were the very ones for whom Jeremiah had prayed before the Lord.

Difficult though unselfish service is, it is what Jesus requires of us, and he teaches that true greatness comes from serving the needs of others without thought of compensation. Reward there will be, but that we must leave in the hands of God.

Alternate Reflection

Almost everyone enjoys a good meal, but if you are not a cook it may be difficult for you to appreciate all the time and hard work that go into preparing a really fine dinner. It seems that it is necessary to pay some kind of price for all good things, and apparently that is what James and John and their mother in today's gospel had forgotten. The two brothers wanted a share in the kingdom and the glory of Christ, the very place of honor, but our Lord had to remind them that there was a price to be paid. It was the price he himself had to pay for his glorification, namely his passion and death.

Jesus warned all the apostles that he had to go up to Jerusalem to suffer and die, and only then would he be raised to glory and come into the possession of his kingdom.

On several occasions our Lord likened his kingdom to a great banquet. In this Mass, the Eucharistic banquet, we have an anticipation of the heavenly banquet, but with this spiritual meal we are also reminded of the price to be paid. Christ is present as our food in this Mass only because he first makes himself present as a victim through the sacred sign of the consecration. We receive communion, a sharing in the resurrection of Christ, with the best dispositions only if we first identify ourselves with him as the victim of sacrifice. That identity means the total dedication of ourselves to God with Christ, even to death. Can we indeed drink of the cup of the Lord?

THURSDAY OF THE SECOND WEEK

Jeremiah 17, 5-10

Chapter 17 is a collection of various sayings, two of which appear here. In vv. 5-8 there is a comparison between those who trust in God and those who trust in men. In the dry Near East a tree that is not near a source of water never gets beyond bush size and dies when the rains cease and the heat comes. In the same way the man who forsakes God and puts his trust in another man removes himself from the source of life. But he who keeps his trust in God is like a green tree near a source of water from which it continually draws and is not harmed by the dry hot season. He constantly has strength to endure. God is man's sole refuge. Verses 9-10 point out that if the deceits of the human heart are hidden from other men, God knows them and punishes accordingly.

Luke 16, 19-31

This is one of Luke's two-pronged parables addressed to the Pharisees "who were fond of money" (v. 14). The lesson taught by the first part of the parable is the evil consequence of the mishandling of money: eternal separation from the eschatological banquet in the company of Abraham. The sin of the rich man is not in what he did with his money but his blind indifference to the plight of the poor. Now suffering the consequences of his life the rich man pleads with Abraham to send Lazarus to warn his brothers so that they will not make the same mistake. Abraham, in his response, brings out the second and more important point of the parable: Moses and the prophets have pointed out the way of salvation and if the Pharisees will not listen to them no sign is going to be of any use.

Reflection

The Pharisees, to whom today's parable was originally directed, are described in the gospel as being "fond of money." Our Lord also referred to them as "blind guides," and it was their fondness for money that made them spiritually blind to their neighbors, as well as deaf to the word of God.

Our Lord's object in the parable was not to condemn wealth as such but to point up the evil consequences of its abuse. The rich man dressed in finery and pampered his appetite for exquisite food and drink. He was so taken up with his own pleasures that he failed to pay any attention to poor Lazarus starving at his gate. In his condition Lazarus would have considered the scraps from the rich man's table a banquet but not even the scraps were offered to him. The rich man had allowed his wealthy circumstances to blind him to the need of others.

Secondly, abuse of wealth had induced spiritual deafness. From the abode of the dead, the rich man pleaded with Abraham to send Lazarus to warn his five brothers. Abraham answered, "They have Moses and the prophets. Let them hear them." Abraham then went on to say that if the brothers have been deaf to the word of God found in Moses and the prophets, they would not be converted even if one should rise from the dead.

Wealth is enticing because of the pleasures it can bring. But the man who lives for pleasure alone will wither and dry up like the barren bush described in today's first lesson. The person who keeps his eyes open to the needs of others and listens attentively to the word of God will be like the tree planted near running water. He will yield good fruit, a fruit that will endure unto everlasting life.

Alternate Reflection

There is a paradox about poverty in the New Testament. On the one hand Jesus tells us that a poor man is fortunate. On the other hand he tells us that we should help to overcome the poverty of others. How can this be?

The point is that Jesus wants us to be free. Freedom is the key to the whole question of both poverty and wealth. If we are attached to material things, we can lose our freedom. Look at the rich man in today's gospel. He wore fine clothes and enjoyed a splendid banquet every day, but apparently he was so wrapped up in his pleasures that he had no time for God or for his fellow men. He had lost his freedom because of his attachment to wealth and the pleasures that wealth brought him. He would have been better off if he had been poor.

And yet being poor can be a problem for freedom too. We need God's material gifts in order to have the leisure of time and mind to worship God and be concerned about others. If a person has to spend all his time and effort in trying to acquire the very basic necessities of survival and has to actually wonder where his next meal is coming from, he can scarcely turn his attention to God or the needs of others. He has lost his freedom because of a poverty which is destitution.

It is unlikely that any of us here is either destitute or extremely wealthy. But how free are we? If we are neither destitute nor wealthy, are we satisfied with moderation, or deep in our hearts are we constantly yearning for more and more? A good test is to see what are the things we usually pray for. Another good test is to examine how generous is our charity in helping others. The rich man in today's gospel was condemned not because he was wealthy but because he was selfish. He was not willing to share even the scraps from his table with the poor man. How really free are we?

FRIDAY OF THE SECOND WEEK

Genesis 37, 3-4, 12-13a, 17b-28

> The saying "God writes straight with crooked lines" brings out well the point of the Joseph story (Gn 37-50), the beginning of which we read today. The story stands out because of its lack of divine interventions and special revelations which usually mark the narratives in Genesis. Here we see that God can work out his will through the ordinary course of human events. The evil plottings of the brothers will eventually bring about the salvation of Jacob's family. Joseph's brothers hate him and plan to kill him because of the special love shown him by their father,

Jacob. Joseph's deliverance from death is presented in two different accounts woven together. In one it is Judah who saves him by persuading his brothers to sell him to some passing Ishmaelite traders. In the other it is Reuben who protects him by having him put in an empty cistern so as to rescue him later. Meanwhile Midianite traders pass by and take Joseph to Egypt.

Matthew 21, 33-43, 45-46

This parable, which has its inspiration in Is 5, 2f, has allegorical details. The vineyard is Israel; the tenants are the leaders of Israel; the servants are the prophets; the son is Jesus himself. The point of the parable is clear: since the Jews have rejected the prophets sent by God and even Jesus himself, they have forfeited their status as God's chosen people and the kingdom will be given over to others. In the context the "others" are certainly the Gentiles (see Mt 21, 28-32). To this parable the early Church added the quotation from Ps 118 in v. 42: He who was rejected by Israel has become the cornerstone of a new edifice, the Church. The episode ends with the chief priests and Pharisees understanding that he had spoken of them. They would have arrested him, but for the moment his popularity was too great.

Reflection

The brothers of Joseph in today's lesson were guilty of envy. They were saddened and even angered because of the favors received by Joseph, and they looked upon his good fortune as a threat to themselves. The evil men in the gospel parable were also guilty of envy. When they saw the property owner's son, they said, "Let us kill him and then we shall have his inheritance!"

Perhaps surprisingly, envy is a vice that even good people can sometimes be guilty of. If we are really trying to be good Christians, we may be led to wonder why it is that others seem to be more favored than we are by God and the circumstances of life. The problem is intensified if we see someone who does not seem to be a particularly good person prospering and enjoying comfort and security. It can even hurt us to hear someone else praised, especially if we think that maybe we deserve a little praise once in a while.

Of course envy is born of pride and selfishness. What we have to remember is that we are all children of God, that we are all brothers united in Christ and forming one body with him. As St. Paul teaches about the mystical body of Christ, the good qualities and achievements of one member help all the other members. What we are all working for ulti-mately is the glory of God, who gives us his gifts so that we may glorify him. In the final analysis, it is God's business to whom he gives his gifts.

At Mass today let us humble ourselves before God our Father. Let us thank him for his gifts to us, and ask him to give us the grace to be big enough to be happy that he also gives his gifts to others.

Alternate Reflection

There is an old saying that God can write straight with crooked lines. It is a comment which fits the story of Joseph in the Old Testament which we have just read. Joseph's brothers sold him into slavery. As he was led away to Egypt Joseph did not in any way realize how God would use that evil deed to save his brothers and their families from starvation. You know the touching story of how Joseph res-cued his people during a time of famine after he had come to great authority in Egypt.

The same comment can be made about today's parable from the New Testament. The son, murdered by the tenant farmers, represents Jesus himself. The farmers through their evil deed hoped to have the son's inheritance. As a matter of fact the death of Jesus brought the grace of his heavenly inheritance to the whole world. God used the malice of some men to bring supreme good to all mankind.

We sometimes wonder where God's plan is to be found. We see natural disasters, riots, and war itself as part of our world. In our own personal lives we experience sickness, suffering, and frustration. At the moment, like Joseph, we cannot see why God tolerates all these evils, let alone how he will use them to accomplish his good purposes. But we must never be fooled into suspecting that somehow God has lost control of human affairs or that evil has become so powerful that even God cannot draw good from it. Though it is true that God could prevent all evil, in his supreme wisdom and for his own good reasons he has chosen to write straight with crooked lines.

SATURDAY OF THE SECOND WEEK

Micah 7, 14-15, 18-20

A prayer which concludes the book of Micah. It probably comes from the time after the exile when the Jews were trying to rehabilitate themselves. In the first part of the prayer (14-15) they ask the Lord to once again give them the fat pasture land of Basan and Galaad (in the Transjordan area) and bring them out of the wooded hills. In the second part of the prayer (18-20) Israel praises Yahweh as the God who forgives, who does not stay angry, and she places her trust in his forgiveness. For he had sworn his faithfulness and mercy to the Israel of old and certainly he will honor his oath now.

Luke 15, 1-3, 11-32

The Pharisees were scandalized over Jesus' association with sinners and publicans. Jesus answers them with this parable. The emphasis in the parable is on the loving father. When the younger son returned, repentant, the father rushed out to meet him and poured out on him every honor. The point is God's great happiness over the return of the sinner and the incredible mercy he is ready to confer on such a one. But the parable is two-pronged with the greater emphasis on the second point. The story continues with the lack of understanding of the elder son who represents the Pharisees who never "disobeyed one of your orders." He is angry over the treatment his father has shown to his younger brother. But the father gently points out to him that he has remained his heir and tells him that he too should rejoice over his brother's return. The message is clear: the Pharisees should also rejoice over God's reception of sinners and not stay enclosed in their own self-righteousness.

Reflection

Our Lord told the parable we have just heard because the scribes and the Pharisees had complained about his kind treatment of known sinners. By his parable he wanted to show that he was doing his Father's will in seeking out sinners to save them. The scribes and the Pharisees, had they been really good men, would have been glad to see sinners being led to repentance. In the parable they are represented by the older son who, by his own estimate anyway, had remained loyal to his father. This older son, however, was guilty of envy, and his father had to point out to him that he too should have rejoiced over the return of his brother. The younger brother had indeed been foolish in his sin, but the older brother was equally foolish in his self-righteousness and envy.

Where do we fit into the parable? Probably we do not completely match either son, but are a little bit like both of them. We certainly should realize that we are not perfect, that we are guilty of some sins, usually little ones but maybe serious ones at some time. During Lent we are expected in a special way to be honest about our sins. Whatever our sins may be, we know from this par   that God is a loving

Father who welcomes back the repentant sinner with open arms.

In comparison with people whom some would be tempted to label as notorious sinners, we may look like saints. It may even be that a close friend or member of our family or a priest we have known has left the Church. In relation to such people we are in danger of acting like the older son of the parable, and so we must not fall into the sin of self-righteousness. If others have wandered away from their Father's home, they should be our concern. We should be praying for them. We should even attempt to search them out to lead them back to God. It certainly should be a source of great joy to know that a person has repented.

Whichever son we may resemble at the moment, at all times we must remember that God loves all his children and welcomes them with open arms.

Alternate Reflection

The story of the prodigal son is a parable; though it is not factual, it is in accord with the truth, and the truth it teaches has been manifested in the lives of many throughout the centuries. Here is a factual story which reflects that truth.

A child was born of devout parents. As a young man, however, he not only left home but also abandoned any attachment to the true faith. He lived what we would call a wild life and even fathered a son out of wedlock. One person stood by him, his mother. She never gave up praying for him. At her insistent urging he listened to the preaching of a very holy bishop. Struck by the preaching and influenced by his mother's prayers, he realized the mistakes he had made and changed his whole way of life. His conversion was so complete that he founded a religious order, was made a bishop, and became a famous preacher, writer, and theologian of the Church. At his mother's funeral he said in his sermon, "I weep for my mother, now dead before my sight, who wept for me for so many years that I might live in her sight." We now honor this man every year in the liturgy on August 28th as the great St. Augustine.

St. Monica, Augustine's mother, never gave up on him, just as God never gives up anyone, whether they be big sinners or little sinners. During Lent the Church calls us to repentance and like a good mother weeps for our sins and prays for our conversion. Though we have not abandoned our Father's home, we must do penance for all our sins, big or small, and we must try to cooperate with the grace of God who wishes to raise us even to the heights of sanctity.

OPTIONAL MASS FOR THE THIRD WEEK

Exodus 17, 1-7

This incident of the rock which gives forth water when struck by Moses must be seen in the context of the Israelites' journey to Sinai after coming out of Egypt. This journey is presented through a series of anecdotes that tell of God's care for his people. A theme that runs through these stories is the grumbling of the people against Moses and God. The point that is brought out many times over is not only that God cares for his people but that God will carry out his plan of salvation despite the adversity of the elements and the recalcitrance of the people. Israel grumbles here because of their lack of water. Moses is blamed for the problem and he in turn sees their grumbling as a putting of the Lord to the proof. But God provides once again.

John 4, 5-42

The main theme is Jesus' increasing self-revelation. At first the woman only sees in him a Jew. Then, through Johannine irony, Jesus is spoken of as one who is greater than Jacob. This is the result of Jesus' offer of "living water," i.e., his revelation and the Spirit who interprets this revelation to men. The woman does not understand. He leads her to a deeper understanding by referring to her personal life. Then she recognizes him as a prophet and asks him for the solution to a burning question, the true place of worship. In his response Jesus speaks of the manner of worship and reveals that with his coming the only worship the Father seeks is that done by those who possess the Spirit. It is the Spirit who allows men to worship God properly. Now she recognizes him as the Messiah. To the returning disciples Jesus reveals his mission: "doing the will of him who sent me...." The Samaritans, upon hearing his word, profess him to be the Savior of the world.

Reflection

In their exodus from Egypt and their passage through the waters of the Red Sea, the Israelites were formed into the people of God. Despite their grumbling and recalcitrance during their journey to the promised land, God sustained them with the manna from heaven and the water from the rock.

We as Christians are formed into the people of God by our passage through the waters of baptism and on our journey to heaven God sustains us with the food and drink of the Eucharist.

The *Constitution on the Church* of Vatican II emphasizes that we are a pilgrim people, a people on a journey to our true home, which is heaven (cf. ch. 7). During our journey we are somewhat like the Israelites in their journey to the promised land. We can get discouraged, tired, hungry, and thirsty. The Israelites longed for food, and God strengthened them with the manna from heaven. They yearned for drink, and God refreshed them with water from the rock. We have our strength and refreshment in Jesus. In today's gospel he says, "The water I give will become a fountain, leaping up to provide eternal life." Through the symbol of water Jesus was referring to his grace. We receive this grace chiefly in the food and drink of the Eucharist, a nourishment that will lead us through this life to the eternal life of heaven.

At Mass you come in procession to the altar to receive the Eucharist. This procession is a sign that we are on a journey to heaven, and we come to the altar to receive the food of pilgrims. The Eucharist will indeed strengthen us and bring us home to heaven, our promised land.

MONDAY OF THE THIRD WEEK

2 Kings 5, 1-15a

See the optional Mass for the fifth week. The word "leprosy" covered various kinds of skin diseases. The King of Israel suspects a plot when Naaman comes with his letter. Elisha's aloof attitude, in that he did not come out personally to see Naaman, may be explained as a testing of the faith of Naaman or simply Elisha's standing on his pride: if Naaman would not deign to enter Elisha's house, Elisha would not go out to meet him. Naaman, upset at his peremptory treatment and expecting something a bit more dramatic, is nevertheless persuaded by his servants to follow the prophet's advice and is cured. Naaman professes his faith in Yahweh as God alone. In the New Testament this story is used to prefigure the call of the gentiles to the messianic kingdom (Lk 4, 27).

Luke 4, 24-30

Luke places the rejection of Jesus by his own townspeople right at the beginning of his ministry to show the pattern the ministry is to follow. The announcement of Jesus that the messianic age had begun was at first excitedly received (4, 14-22a). But then doubts began to set in for they saw him only as the son of Joseph and they could not conceive of him as being anything greater: "no prophet gains acceptance in his native place." When Jesus suggested, by means of his references to Elijah (1 K 17-18) and Elisha (2 K 5), that his ministry would eventually include the gentiles he was met with mob violence. They were about to kill him but no one dared to hurt him when the decisive moment came. The pattern is set: Jesus will be rejected by his own and the call will go out to the gentiles. The following incident (4, 31-44) will show his enthusiastic reception by outsiders.

Reflection

One of the most common failures of our human condition is to take things for granted, especially those which have become very familiar to us or which are very simple.

Jesus was rejected by the people of his home town of Nazareth because he was too familiar to them and his background too simple; they took him for granted. As we read in today's lesson, Elisha's directions to Naaman for the cure of his leprosy were at first spurned by Naaman because they seemed too simple and commonplace.

There is a real danger that we may take the Mass for granted because it seems so familiar and so simple to us. Actually the Mass is a wonderful experience. To help make it such, I have some suggestions.

As you drive or walk to church, or in the few moments you may have before Mass begins, make the effort to impress on yourself what is about to happen. Say to yourself: "God is about to speak to me in the scriptures, and I will speak to God in the prayers. Jesus will make the great sacrifice of the cross truly present on this altar and he will give me the opportunity, with my fellow Catholics here, to join with him in this offering to the Father. Then I will receive Jesus in holy communion as a pledge of my own resurrection as well as a means of strength to carry on until the day of resurrection." It will take you even less time to make this reflection than it takes me to say it now.

Then when Mass is over spend a moment or two in reflecting on what has happened, to try to realize that you must strive to live a life in accord with the offering of yourself to God. The Mass, simple and familiar though it be, is just too important to take for granted.

Alternate Reflection

There is one day in our lives which we usually consider pretty important, and that is our birthday. It would be a very rare person indeed who would not know the date of his own birth or who would not celebrate that day. As we grow older we may not be too eager to count how many birthdays we have had, but we still like to be greeted with a "happy birthday" from relatives and friends.

Actually we have two birthdays, one when we were born of our parents, and one when we were born of God in baptism. The event related in the first lesson puts us in mind of the sacrament of baptism. Naaman suffered from leprosy. He was asked to do a simple thing by Elisha, to wash seven times in the water of the Jordan. After some reluctance he complied, and, as we saw, he was cured of his leprosy. It was a great day for Naaman, one he never forgot.

Our baptism was a very simple ceremony: a little water was poured over our heads, but it was a great day for us. Not only were we cured of the leprosy of sin, but more importantly God gave us a share in his divine life, and thereby made us his children. It was indeed our spiritual birthday.

It does not really matter too much, I suppose, if we do not know the actual day when we were baptized, but we certainly should celebrate the day with great joy and happiness.

As you know, during Lent there is an emphasis on baptism, an emphasis which reaches its climax in the renewal of our baptism on Holy Saturday. Each time, however, that we come into church we should reflect on our baptism as we take holy water at the font, a symbol of baptism. Then as we see others in the church we should realize that we are all here in our Father's home, brothers and sisters of one another because of our spiritual birth from a common Father in baptism. Indeed, the day of our baptism was a great day for us, one we should never forget.

TUESDAY OF THE THIRD WEEK

Daniel 3, 25, 34-43

    Part of the prayer of the three youths in the fiery furnace. This prayer is a later addition to the text of Daniel for it is a lamentation of the Jewish community rather than of the three youths. But they can be seen as a symbol of the community which was being persecuted c. 165 B.C. The prayer begins (26-33) with the community confessing that it is their sins which have brought on these sufferings. God is called on to remember his covenant with their fathers in which he promised to deliver Israel from her sufferings and make them a great nation (34-36). Their present condition in no way lives up to those promises (37-38). They ask God to accept their sufferings in place of the sacrifices in the temple (39-40) and conclude with a promise to do God's will and a request for deliverance (41-43).

Matthew 18, 21-35

    The discourse in Mt 18, 1-35, deals with the relations between the members of the Church. In vv. 21-35 the specific question is that of forgiveness of personal offenses. The number seven symbolizes perfection. Hence, Peter is asking if there is some definite number of times at which forgiveness becomes perfect so that one no longer is held to forgive if the offense continues. The answer of Christ means that there is no limitation on charity, no number of times makes forgiveness perfect.

The following parable reinforces the idea of forgiveness by giving
its motivation: if God's mercy towards us has been so great
then we ought to forgive our brothers whose offenses are in-
significant in comparison to our offenses against God. We cannot expect forgiveness from God if we do not forgive our brother.

Reflection

A man lay on his death bed. Having held public office,
though never any major ones, he had experienced how a
politician's motives and actions are open to the sometimes
erroneous judgment of others. Despite his good intentions,
he had made many enemies. After his confession, he said to
the priest, "Father, I am grateful for one thing, that I will
be judged by God and not by my fellow men."

The dying man had a point. Though we may fear to
stand before God as our judge, we must remember that God
is not only infinitely wise and powerful, but also infinitely
merciful. His mercy exceeds any mercy a human being could
possibly manifest. Notice in today's parable a detail you
may have overlooked. The official, who owed the huge
amount, pleaded with the master only for a delay; he said,
"My lord, be patient with me and I will pay you back in
full." The master not only heeded the plea but granted even
more than the official dared ask: "Moved with pity, the
master let the official go and *wrote off the debt.*"

The master of course represents God, who wishes to write
off our debt of sin completely, but he will do so only if we
learn to forgive those who have offended us. When our
brother has wronged us, how often must we forgive him?
Jesus says, "Seventy times seven times," that is, without any
limit. When we are tempted to feel that enough is enough,
maybe it will help to remember that any injury done us is
trifling in comparison with the sins we have committed

against God, as the gospel says, a mere fraction.

Like the dying man, we too can be grateful that we w. be judged by God, but only if we have learned to forgive ou brothers without limit from our heart.

Alternate Reflection

Sin is a terrible evil because it offends God. We cannot even begin to imagine how bad sin is because we cannot appreciate how good God is. And yet we know that when we have sinned we can go to confession and have our sins forgiven, no matter how serious or frequent the sin may be. But God does warn us that his forgiveness depends on whether we forgive others from the heart.

Is it not true that we sometimes find it hard to forgive others? Someone says something behind your back. You find out about it. Your indignation grows, and the more you think about it the less inclined you are to forgive this "enemy" of yours. Or someone insults you in front of others, or ignores you, or stands you up for an appointment. It may not seem important to anyone else, but it is important to you and you find the offense hard to forgive.

It is not surprising that we find it hard to forgive. That is the way human nature is. You see, it takes bigness to forgive. That is why it is easy for God to forgive, difficult for us. Jesus understood all this, and so he told the parable in today's gospel in order to motivate us to find the bigness needed for forgiveness. The official owed a huge amount; his master wrote off the whole debt, when merely asked for a delay, because he was a big man. But that same official could not forgive a small debt owed him by a fellow servant because he himself was a small man.

Any offense against us is a mere fraction of what we are

guilty of by sin before God. The lesson of today's parable is strikingly clear: if we want forgiveness from God we must forgive those who have offended us.

WEDNESDAY OF THE THIRD WEEK

Deuteronomy 4, 1, 5-9

In chs. 1-3 we find a summary of the events between Horeb, where God gave the Law to Moses, and the conquest of the Transjordan. In ch. 4 we have an exhortation by Moses to keep the Law. It is a plea for Israel to respond to these saving acts of Yahweh on her behalf by giving him their allegiance and love through the observance of the Law. There are two reasons why Israel should keep the Law: first, the Law is a source of life and so if they keep it they will live; second, the Law is of divine origin and a source of wisdom, i.e., it gives the ability to recognize the true values of life. The Law, then, is not a burden, but another expression of God's love for Israel for he is a God who is always close at hand.

Matthew 5, 17-19

The context is the Sermon on the Mount. In the preceding section Jesus told his disciples of their duty to glorify God through their good works and now he explains what these good works are (5, 17-48). First, he sets forth the principle (17-20) which will be illustrated by six examples. The point is this: good works are not merely the external observance of the letter of the Law. Certainly, the Law is an expression of God's will for men. But it is an imperfect expression as all human words must necessarily be. What Jesus wants is for man to get to the spirit of the Law as it is expressed through these imperfect utterances. This spirit of the Law is found in the law of love of God and neighbor (cf. Mt 7, 12; 22, 40). This is the revelation of Christ and the way he "fulfills" the Law. So one is not to do away with the Law but to act according to the spirit of the Law.

Reflection

We all realize that the purpose behind traffic laws is to provide for the safety of both motorists and pedestrians. Merely sticking to the letter of the law, however, can get you into trouble. For example, say someone runs through a stop sign when you have the right of way. The law is, strictly speaking, on your side, but insisting on your right of way at that moment may well be the way to an accident, perhaps even death itself. The spirit behind the law, not to mention common sense, would demand that you stop.

This illustration is close to the idea our Lord had in mind in today's gospel. He said that he had not come to abolish the law found in the Old Testament. That law was an expression of God's will for people, but because it was necessarily put in human words it was an imperfect expression of God's will. The spirit behind the law is what counts, and that spirit is found in the love of God and the neighbor. Jesus fulfilled the law first by his more complete teaching on love, and secondly by his own supreme example of love. It is his teaching and example that Jesus wants us to follow, and not merely the letter of the law.

For instance, no law requires that you be present at Mass on weekdays during Lent. But in the celebration of these Masses you are certainly fulfilling the spirit behind the command that we love God and pray to him. You won't find any explicit law which says that if your neighbor down the block has just come home from the hospital you must go and find out what help you can be, but taking the initiative in a case like that is in accord with the spirit of the law. If a friend of yours has abandoned the church because of, say, an argument with his pastor there is no precise legislation requiring that you be the one to try to straighten him out. The spirit of the law, however, should motivate you to approach your friend with understanding and affection.

Perhaps a twist of John F. Kennedy's famous words from his inaugural address fits the idea: Ask not what the law demands that you do, but ask what you can do to fulfill the spirit of the law.

Alternate Reflection

Do you remember not long ago when there were as many ads on television against smoking as there were commercials pushing different brands of cigarettes? One episode showed a father walking down a country road with his young son. Everything the father did the little boy imitated: throwing a rock, admiring a bird, and stretching in the marvelous sunshine. Then the father sat by a tree and his son did the same. The punch of the ad came as the father took a cigarette, lay the pack on the ground, and the little boy slowly reached for the pack.

What we do, the way we live, the example we set, all influence others, adults as well as children. We would probably be amazed if we were to know how much we do affect others. Jesus says in today's gospel, "Whoever breaks the least significant of these commands and teaches others to do so shall be called least in the kingdom of God." What a terrible thing it would be deliberately to teach evil to others. We hope and pray that we will never become so perverse. But we teach others not only by our words but also by our example. As a matter of fact, we recognize, at least in theory, that "actions speak louder than words." Someone put it another way when he said, "What you are speaks so loudly that I cannot hear what you say."

Some people maintain that they do not go to church because churchgoers are hypocrites. Such a position usually is an excuse to hide some deeper problem, but there is a good point here nonetheless. Our lives do have an influence on others, for good or ill. If our example "fulfills and teaches God's commands we shall be great in the kingdom of God."

THURSDAY OF THE THIRD WEEK

Jeremiah 7, 23-28

Today's reading is part of one of several oracles added on by an editor to Jeremiah's famous "Temple Sermon." In 7, 21-28, the prophet condemns the people for trying to satisfy Yahweh's demands by means of external cultic practices. Yahweh's essential demand is for a genuine attitude of obedience to the stipulations of the covenant. Without such an internal obedience all of their external sacrifices are meaningless and have no value before God. The Lord has constantly sent his prophets to warn the people on this point but they paid no attention and remained obstinate in their disobedience. Nor will they listen to Jeremiah, says the Lord, for they no longer know what it means to be faithful.

Luke 11, 14-23

Jesus casts out a demon from a man who is dumb. Miracles are an attack upon Satan since sickness is seen to be the result of Satan's hold on the human race. But Jesus is accused of casting out demons by the power of Satan. Jesus responds by pointing out that Satan is not a fool and so is not about to allow dissension among his followers. Also, disciples of the Pharisees themselves cast out demons. Are their powers to be ascribed to Satan? If not, then why do they deny that God is also working through him. They ask for signs (16) but the expulsion of demons is the sign that the Kingdom of God is now operating in the world in the works of Jesus. They should recognize, as did the Egyptians, in the face of the miracles of Moses and Aaron (Ex 8, 15-19), that only the finger of God can work such miracles.

Satan's power has now been broken. The coming of the Kingdom and the attack on Satan by Jesus demands that men take sides in the conflict.

Reflection

The history of our world is to a large extent the story of war, lust, greed, and selfishness. What is behind it all? To-day's gospel, as well as much of sacred scripture, implies that it is the devil. Many people say that believing that there is a devil is naïve and childish, but the truth is that not accepting the reality of the devil is naïve and childish. The Bible teaches that there are intelligent, highly powerful forces for evil in the world, known as devils. That teaching is in accord with reality.

Look at Nazism and all its horrors: millions of people exterminated. How could any human being ever wish such evil? Adolf Hitler was no doubt insane, but maybe part of the cause of his insanity was the power of Satan. Communism began with a certain sincerity and good intention on the part of Marx and Lenin, but how did it become such a mon-ster today?

The devil puts ideas into people's heads under the guise that the ideas represent freedom and goodness. Look at the attack on human life in the movements for abortion, eutha-nasia, and compulsory sterilization. Or look at the blows dealt to human dignity in today's sexual revolution: pre-marital sex, wife swapping, the disintegration of marriage and the family.

Christianity does not mean no fun; it is not a religion for prudes, such as the scribes and the Pharisees in the gospel who were just waiting for Christ to do something wrong so that they could pounce on him. But we must make no mistake about the fact that there is a war going on, a war between good and evil, between Christ and the devil. Our Lord warns us today that we must take sides. We simply cannot fool around with the important issues of morality. If we are not for Christ and his teaching, then we are against him.

Alternate Reflection

Before our baptism we were, in a sense, like the mute in today's gospel. We were freed from the power of the devil by the grace of our baptism. Jesus warns however that the devil is strong, and that if we are not constantly on our guard he will overpower us. The devil we rejected in our baptism is insidious and persistent in trying to claim us for himself. Our only defense is to fill the void left by the devil with the love of God and the neighbor.

The devil these days uses many different weapons in the hope of destroying Christian love in our hearts. One is rugged individualism, which in its false independence and pride refuses to see the necessity of depending on God for anything. Another is materialism, which considers the accumulation of possessions and power as the goal of life, and not the love of God. Still a third weapon is indifference, which makes the Christian either unaware of the needs of others, or unconcerned with helping to meet those needs. Last to be mentioned here is the subtle yet extremely effective weapon of smug complacency, which makes the Christian feel, as did the people addressed in today's first lesson, that simply because he is baptized and has the faith his eternal salvation is assured, and that nothing more need be done except to fufill the mere letter of the law. This last weapon is frequently the first to be used by the devil to get his foot in the door, for then he can utilize the destructive force of rugged individualism, materialism, and indifference to their fullest extent.

Jesus warns that if we are strong "our possessions will go undisturbed." Our greatest strength comes from an unselfish, generous love of God and the neighbor.

FRIDAY OF THE THIRD WEEK

Hosea 14, 2-10

This passage concludes the book of Hosea and offers a message of hope for it shows what can happen if Israel will sincerely turn to the Lord. First, the prophet calls on the people to return to their God (2-4). But a true return demands more than just external cult. Accompanying the sacrifices must be true repentance expressed in words that come from the heart. This is the good that will give the sacrifices value because they will then represent true devotion. A sample of what they should say then follows: Israel is to admit her guilt and reject all her political alliances, her military forces, and her idols. Yahweh's answer (5-9) then comes through the prophet: He will heal them and out of his love, which is freely given and not earned, he will make them beautiful and grant them all they need.

Mark 12, 28b-34

During the last week of his life Jesus is pictured by Mark as engaged in controversy with the representatives of Judaism (11, 27-12, 37). This incident, however, portrays a friendly discussion. The purpose of the episode is to emphasize the essential orthodoxy of Jesus and his faithfulness to the Law just as the rift between himself and the Jewish leaders is reaching its climax. The rabbis argued about which was the great commandment from which all the others could be deduced. In the view of Jesus it is the law of love of God and neighbor. In the Old Testament the law of love of God was seen as one of the possible formulations of the great commandment. Jesus takes over

this particular formulation and combines it with love of neighbor into a single moral principle, identifying love of God and
love of neighbor. The scribe agrees with Jesus and points out
the primacy of love over even ritual sacrifice. For without such
love ritual sacrifice has no value.

Reflection

The question asked by the scribe in today's gospel about
the greatest commandment was not an idle one. The rabbis
of the time had determined that there were 613 distinct commandments in the law, and they distinguished not only between great and small commandments, but even *very* great
and *very* small ones. Moreover, some people lived according to what was an observance of merely the letter of the law
without regard for its spirit, despite the warnings of the
prophets throughout the history of Israel that external cult
was insufficient.

The answer of Jesus, to love God and love the neighbor,
not only indicated the greatest commandment, but also revealed the spirit and purpose behind all of the other commandments of the law. We are so familiar with this teaching
of Jesus that we may fail to see its vital import for our lives.

Today in the Church we have gotten away from a lot of
very small rules. and obligations, which had their value at
certain times and places. Some of you will remember when
the fast before communion was so stringent that you dared
not brush your teeth before Mass lest you accidentally swal-
low even a drop of water. There was a time too when you
would not eat pork and beans on a Friday because of the
almost minuscule amount of meat contained in them. And
before you would reach almost any moral decision, you first
consulted a priest. Today we enjoy a greater freedom, and
we know that the Spirit is at work in all of us.

One lesson to be drawn from today's gospel is that our freedom must be exercised to allow for a greater love of God and our neighbor. The validity of any movement we think we feel from the Spirit is to be confirmed by how conducive that movement is to loving God and the neighbor more unselfishly.

As mature people we all want to enjoy freedom and do not wish to be restrained like children by a whole host of petty rules and regulations. Our freedom will be really mature and responsible if we learn to live according to the great command to love God and our neighbor. And then, like the scribe in today's gospel, we too will not be far from the reign of God.

Alternate Reflection

St. John the Apostle lived to a very old age. Toward the end of his life he was so feeble that he had to be carried to the church. Though he could not preach at length because of his advanced age, he insisted on saying something at Mass. His message was brief and it was always the same: "My children, love one another." Everybody was bored with the sameness of his words, and finally someone got up enough courage to ask, "Master, why do you always say the same thing?" John patiently and calmly replied, "Because it is the command of the Lord; if only this is done, it is enough."

St. John was indeed imitating Jesus who never wearied of preaching the command of love, a command which we have heard once again in today's gospel. To love God and love the neighbor is the greatest commandment of all. Our Lord never tired of repeating it; we must never tire of hearing it, because there is certainly a great need for love in our world. As a popular song put it, "What the world needs too little of."

John was right in saying, "If only this is done, it is enough."

If love were the controlling force on this earth, there would be no wars, no riots, no injustices. We know that we are far from this ideal. Where do we start? I think the answer is obvious. We must start within the framework of our personal lives. "Charity begins at home"—that is, with the persons we live with and work with every day. There is no point in complaining about the lack of love that produces wars and riots and injustice if love is not the motivating force in our personal lives. And the Lord knows that there is a lot more room for love in the lives of each one of us.

In coming to Church you will again and again hear about the command of love. You must never tire of hearing it, and you must never give up trying to practice it. "It is the command of the Lord; if only this is done, it is enough."

SATURDAY OF THE THIRD WEEK

Hosea 6, 1-6
    Israel, suffering because of her sins, sought help in political alliances with foreign nations. But then she recognized her suffering as a punishment from Yahweh and once again turned to him (1-3). But her repentance is insincere, or at least insufficient, for it is prompted only by affliction and is presumptuous. The people are convinced that God will only punish for a short time and that no matter how insincere their repentance he will pardon them with a regularity that parallels the seasonal rains ("two days . . . third day": a short time, not a definite period). He will restore their health ("raise us up") so they will not be separated from him in death. But Yahweh is not satisfied with their return for it is devoid of a real internal change. They think they can satisfy him with external cult but what he wants is

love, submission to his will. Without that their sacrifices count
for nothing.

Luke 18, 9-14

The point of this parable is the nature of true prayer and
is addressed to those "who believed in their own self-righteousness while holding everyone else in contempt." First, there is
given an example of what prayer should not be. The Pharisee's
prayer is simply a catalogue of his accomplishments. He is proud
of himself because of his external observance of the Law and
he despises those who have not done as he. Being completely
confident of his own righteousness he asks for nothing from
God and receives nothing. The tax collector, on the other hand,
simply admits his sinfulness, his need for God, and places his
trust in him. Because of his humble attitude God has mercy on
him and justifies him. But the Pharisee, with his trust in his
own external observance of the Law, remains unjustified.

Reflection

A young man was very conscious of the fact that he was
rather short. He made a point of dating only girls who were
much shorter than he so that he could live under the delu-
sion of thinking of himself as being tall. This self-deception,
on a much more serious scale, was one of the problems of
the Pharisee in today's gospel. His prayer, far from being
a humble and honest admission of weakness, was a form of
self-congratulations because he was making the wrong point
of comparison. Rather than comparing himself with people
who had the reputation of being grasping, crooked, and adul-
terous, he should have been comparing himself with God,
who is perfection itself.

We here at Mass today could, I suppose, be thought of as
being better than some people who have no regard for religion or morals. And yet, as we begin every Mass we are
urged to call to mind our sins, and to say, in effect, "O God,

be merciful to me, a sinner." Indeed we are sinners in comparison with the goodness of God. And it is God who should be the point of comparison since Jesus said, "Be perfect as your heavenly Father is perfect."

To stand before God with a humble, honest admission of our imperfection is the key to true, effective prayer. Notice that the Pharisee's "prayer" was a nauseous mixture of pride and self-complacency. He asked for nothing from God, and he received nothing in return. The tax collector asked for mercy and he received justification from God. If our prayer is to be effective, it must begin with a plea for mercy. How sincere, then, should be our prayer, "Lord, have mercy."

Alternate Reflection

These days there are some people who seem to want to excuse all sins. They say that heredity is to blame, or environment, or psychological factors, or something else. Still others maintain that a feeling of sinfulness is a guilt complex, a hang-up. They put one in mind of the man who felt he had a guilt complex and told his psychiatrist so. After spending a long time in many visits with the man, the honest psychiatrist said to him, "You don't have a guilt complex; you are guilty."

Certainly it is true that heredity and environment have influence on us, and a real psychological problem is no laughing matter. But we must remember that the mark of maturity is to accept responsibility for our free actions, not to seek excuses for our mistakes, and that a spiritually healthy person is honest with himself before God, while to deceive oneself habitually and to live in a make-believe world of self-righteousness is to border on mental as well as spiritual illness.

The Pharisee in the parable certainly had no guilt complex; in a sense you might say that he had an innocence complex. Rather than being straightforward and honest, he put forth a catalogue of shallow virtues to cover over the guilt of his deep pride. In contrast the tax collector acted grownup; no excuses, no double talk, just the plain truth about himself as he prayed, "O God, be merciful to me, a sinner."

Of course we should not pretend to have sins, of which we are not guilty, nor should we exaggerate our real sins. But with complete honesty we should admit our sins, and without fear we should turn to Jesus for mercy, who came to call sinners.

OPTIONAL MASS FOR THE FOURTH WEEK

Micah 7, 7-9

Writing at the end of the eighth century B.C., Micah, after lamenting the fact of almost universal iniquity and that no man could be trusted (7, 1-6), turns and puts his trust in God alone. It is God alone who can save (7, 7: this verse may be a later addition by a scribe). Verses 8 and 9 are an act of faith in God by Israel. She acknowledges that her present sufferings are her due punishment because of her sins but she is also sure that the Lord, because of his fidelity to his promises, his justice, will once again turn to her and deliver her from the hands of her enemies and bring her salvation.

John 9, 1-41

The primary purpose of this story is to present a dramatic proof that Jesus is the light of the world who triumphs over darkness and gives eternal life to man. A secondary purpose is to bring out who this Jesus is, if he can work such miracles. The man who was born blind does not doubt that Jesus can work miracles and throughout the story he is shown coming to an ever growing realization of who Jesus is. In the beginning he is simply the "man they call Jesus" (11), then a "prophet" (17), one who is "from God" (33), the "Son of Man" (36), and

finally the "Lord" whom he worships (38). The Pharisees, however, become ever more blind to the truth. They end up prac-
tically denying the miracle, calling Jesus a sinner and con-
fessing that they do not know where he is from nor do they want
to know. In willfully closing their eyes to Jesus they have condemned themselves. The evangelist also intended the healing
itself to be a symbol of baptism.

Reflection

For those of us who enjoy the gift of sight, it is impossible to appreciate what it means to be blind. We can close
our eyes and pretend that we are blind, but of course we
know that all we have to do is to open our eyes in order
to see again.

The primary purpose of today's gospel story was to present a dramatic proof that Jesus is the light of the world who
triumphs over the darkness of sin and gives eternal life to
men. Unfortunately the Pharisees deliberately closed their
eyes to Jesus and in doing so condemned themselves. To be
saved, all they had to do was to open their eyes in order to
see with the same faith that had come to the man born blind.

The early Church saw in the healing of the man born
blind a symbol of baptism, wherein we are healed of the
effects of sin and our eyes are opened in faith to Jesus. In
the ceremony of baptism, a small candle is lit from the paschal candle, which represents Christ. The priest then says,
"This child has been enlightened by Christ. . . . May he
keep the flame of faith alive in his heart. When the Lord
comes, may he go out to meet him with all the saints in the
heavenly kingdom."

During the Holy Saturday service, the paschal candle is
carried into the darkened church as a symbol of the light of
Christ who came into a world darkened by sin. Later in the

service we will all be invited to renew our baptism, to open our eyes to Christ with an even more intense faith in him. As Lent progresses we should look forward to that time of renewal with a prayer that our faith may become stronger day by day.

MONDAY OF THE FOURTH WEEK

Isaiah 65, 17-21

These verses are definitely eschatological. The prophet, in ch. 65, has been contrasting the future of the faithful and God's servants. Here he announces in detail the salvation to come to God's servants. It will be a miraculous transformation of the world. All the universe is to share in man's salvation. All the troubles and sorrows of the past will be forgotten for now joy is to envelop everyone: the people will rejoice in their salvation and God will rejoice in what he has done. There will be no more weeping or premature death nor is there ever again to be any work that is vain and pointless. It is a return to the state of paradise where God is always near and accessible (see vv. 22-25 which continue the picture).

John 4, 43-54

Verses 43-45 are transitional with v. 44 (a later addition) summarizing the Galilean ministry which follows. The Galileans' reception of Jesus is superficial, since it is only a faith in Jesus as a wonder-worker. The main theme of the miracle story is faith. The author wishes to show, through the example of the "royal official," the type of faith the Galileans should have as a result of his signs. At first, the faith of the official, as that of the Galileans, is only a faith that Jesus can work miracles. Jesus rejects this type of faith. But the man persists and believes the word of Jesus. When he hears that his son has been healed and is living he and his household come to full faith in Jesus as the life-giver. This is the type of faith the Galileans should have: a faith in Jesus for what he is, a life-giver, as seen through the signs he works. The life he gives is eternal life. The healing of the boy is a sign of this.

Reflection

Modern medicine in recent times has made tremendous progress. And yet with all its wonders, all that the science of medicine can accomplish at most is to prolong life, to put off the inevitable day of death. It can do nothing once a person has died.

Through his miracles Jesus wanted to show that he had power not only over sickness but over death itself. The faith of the royal official in today's gospel was at first only a belief that Jesus had extraordinary healing powers, that he was some kind of super physician. Jesus rejected that type of faith. But the man struggled, with God's help, to deepen his faith and cried out: "Sir, come down before my child dies." When Jesus told him that his son would live, he put his whole trust in the words of Jesus and started for home. When he discovered upon returning home that his son was alive and well, he came to full faith in Jesus as the life-giver; he became a believer.

This final, complete faith of the official is the kind of faith we must have in Jesus. Jesus is not concerned merely with our temporal well-being. He wishes us to share one day in his own resurrection from the dead, so that we may enjoy his eternal happiness in heaven.

All during Lent we look forward to our celebration at Easter of the resurrection of Jesus from the dead. In faith we must see that Christ's victory over death as manifested in his resurrection is our victory as well. God will one day create new heavens and a new earth, as we heard in the first reading. Provided we keep our faith and trust in Jesus, we will enjoy that new creation through our resurrection with Jesus from the dead.

Alternate Reflection

The royal official of today's gospel was apparently in the service of Herod Antipas. As such he was a rather prominent person in the local community, a man of some dignity and stature in the eyes of the townspeople. Distraught though he was at the serious illness of his son, it must have taken quite a bit of humility for him to admit, first to himself, that things were out of his control, and then to go before the carpenter turned preacher and beg for his help. He had not been a follower of Jesus, one of those who had responded to his message and invitation. He saw in Jesus only a wonder-worker, someone whose help he desperately needed at the moment. It was only later that he became a "believer," that is, a true follower of Jesus.

It is a very natural thing for us to forget all about God, for all practical purposes, when everything is going well for us. But just let something go wrong, and all of a sudden God becomes very important to us. When we need help, we humbly turn to him in prayer. Certainly we should ask God for help, but the prayer of petition does not exhaust our relationship with God. God is more than a super physician or a supreme righter of all wrongs. He is God, the center of our whole lives and one who deserves our prayer of praise and adoration. Our attitude toward God should be like that of the man—you ladies may think him extraordinary—who brings his wife flowers or a box of candy just to show his love. He is not trying to patch up an argument or coax a favor out of his wife. He only wants to let her know what he thinks of her.

A true believer does not think of God only in time of need. He wants to let God know what he thinks of him by means of the prayer of praise and adoration.

TUESDAY OF THE FOURTH WEEK

Ezekiel 47, 1-9, 12

The final section of the book of Ezekiel (40-49) is a picture of the nature of the post-exilic community and its relationship to Yahweh. It is an attempt to say in very concrete terms that God will be present in their midst. First comes a vision of the new Temple, where God dwells, and then a vision of what the new cult will involve. In chs. 47 and 48 there is painted a picture of the effects of this new presence of God in the midst of his people. The world will be transformed into the original state of paradise. The water is a symbol of an abundance of earthly and spiritual blessings, of life. This new life, these blessings, God, once again present among his people, will pour out on his elect and on nature itself so that even the Dead Sea will become a fresh water lake and abound in fish. This river of life-giving water will produce trees of inexhaustible fruitfulness whose leaves will drive away all suffering.

John 5, 1-3a, 5-16

This is the third of the "signs" which reveal Jesus as the one who gives life. In John the miracles of restoring physical health, sight, and life are gifts which symbolize the eternal life which Jesus communicates to man. However, the stress in the story is on the fact that it is the Sabbath. It is Jesus who takes the initiative throughout and nothing is required of the man. He is only asked if he wishes to be healed. The authorities are not interested in the miracle; all they see is a violation of the Sabbath. The man puts the responsibility for the violation on Jesus. The remark of Jesus in the temple is a warning to the man against the worse thing that could happen to him, i.e., the judgment of God, unless his cure brings about a real conversion. It was on account of Jesus' healing people on the Sabbath that the Jewish authorities were actively hostile to him.

Reflection

The first reading today paints a picture of how God will eventually restore this world to its original state of paradise. The water, mentioned so prominently in the prophecy, is a symbol of the abundance of blessings, especially of life it-self, that God will pour out upon his elect.

Perhaps it was this biblical use of water as a symbol of blessings that moved the people of our Lord's day to at-tribute curative powers to the pool of Bethesda. (As a matter of fact the gospel does not assert that the pool had curative power, but only that it was thought to have such.) Jesus took pity on the sick man, apparently a cripple, who clung to a faint hope that the water could restore him to health. With-out recourse to any aid, not even that of the water, Jesus cured the man by his mere word, "Stand up! Pick up your mat and walk!"

When Jesus found the man later in the temple precincts, he said to him, "Give up your sins so that something worse may not overtake you." Jesus did not imply that the man's sickness had been a punishment for sin; rather, he wished to make it clear to the man that sin is worse than any physical ailment, for while his sickness had paralyzed him, sin would lead him to eternal death.

It is good for us to hear this lesson ourselves today. Phys-ical debility and illness are very real and very close to us. If we ourselves are afflicted, or someone we love, the prob-lem and the burden may seem almost overwhelming. But it is not a cliché to say that things could be worse. One seri-ous sin is worse than all the physical suffering in the whole world. Whatever our problem, the words of Jesus are meant for us as well as for the sick man in today's gospel: "Give up your sins so that something worse may not overtake you."

Alternate Reflection

Jesus took pity on the man who had been sick, apparently as a cripple, for thirty-eight years. It was a long time to be sick, but in a moment by the power of his word alone Jesus cured the man. In the confusion caused by the incredible objections of the Pharisees, the man disappeared in the crowd, and it was only later that Jesus found him and said, "Give up your sins." Jesus wanted to make clear to the man that he was interested in his whole well-being, both physical and spiritual. The order of events was different from Jesus' usual practice. Ordinarily he forgave sins before effecting a physical cure.

We can readily understand how Jesus would first be concerned about the sickness of sin. This particular miracle does help to make us realize, however, that indeed it is the whole person whom Jesus wishes to save. Maybe in the past we have put too much emphasis on "saving our souls," almost with the implication that what happens to our bodies does not really matter. As a matter of fact we are God's creature in body as well as soul, and our bodies, if we dare think of them as something separate from our persons, are precious in the eyes of God. Jesus came to save us as whole human beings, not as disembodied souls, and today's miracle is a sign that Jesus' saving grace will bring our whole being to a state of health and happiness.

The mother of Jesus was taken up body as well as soul into heaven, for she did not have to wait for her sharing in the resurrection of Christ. We yearn for the day of the final coming of Christ when he will take us body and soul to heaven to share in his glory.

WEDNESDAY OF THE FOURTH WEEK

Isaiah 49, 8-15
> Deutero-Isaiah here proclaims to Israel in exile that the Lord will once again deliver them on the day he will choose and

bring them back to the land he has given them. This will involve a new exodus during which God will lead them, as a shepherd his flock, protecting them and taking care that all their needs are fulfilled. The elect will come from all directions. There then follows a hymn of praise, the response of the people to God's mercy and saving activity (13). All of creation is to join in this hymn because of the greatness of what God is doing. Israel had been despondent, thinking God had forgotten her, but Yahweh proclaims that where there are limits to human love, his love for Israel goes far beyond even the most tender human love.

John 5, 17-30

The rabbis admitted that God could not rest on the Sabbath or the world would cease to exist. Therefore, says Jesus, as the Father does not cease to work on the Sabbath so neither does the Son. The Jews understand that Jesus is making himself equal to God and this they cannot accept. Jesus replies by insisting on a complete harmony of activity between himself and the Father the source of which is the love of the Father for the Son. Two of the works that he can do as Son of the Father, works which are greater than the two miracles he has just done (4, 43-54; 5, 1-16), are: to grant spiritual life to those dead in sin; to judge men, giving them life or condemnation depending on whether they accept or reject him. He gives this eternal life now to those who believe. Verses 26-30 are another version of 19-25. The latter deal with the theme of Jesus granting life from the aspect of realized eschatology while the former in terms of final eschatology.

Reflection

One of the greatest problems facing the world today is a movement either to deny or ignore the divinity of Christ. There are some who would want to see Jesus as a great philosopher, or social reformer, or even as some kind of beloved beatnik. To be sure, Jesus has a human nature which creates great appeal for us: he graced the wedding banquet, blessed little children, ate and drank with sinners. But Jesus is much more than a man, even a very extraordinary one. He is truly God, and the Jews in today's gospel saw clearly that Jesus spoke of God as his own Father, thereby making himself God's equal.

Jesus forcefully manifested his claim of divinity by attributing to himself two works in particular which are distinctively God's works: these are the greater works which Jesus will show, greater, for instance than the cure of the man at the pool which we heard about in yesterday's gospel. First, Jesus gives life; he raises the dead to life. Secondly, he judges all men, and thereby grants them eternal life or sentences them to eternal condemnation, depending on whether they accept or reject him.

We accept Christ, we believe in his divinity. We should take this occasion to remind ourselves of what this belief entails. It is only by our faith in Christ that we can pass from death to eternal life. It is in Christ that we find God and in him alone. The divine life which God the Father has in himself he has given to us through the Son, by sending him into this world as life-giver and judge. To seek happiness in anyone or anything apart from Jesus is the worst of folly. In Jesus alone is our eternal salvation and our happiness.

Alternate Reflection

There are people who feel that God is very far away from us and completely unconcerned about what is going on in our world. They seem to think that God, after sending us into this world, has lost all interest in us, like some unscrupulous used car salesman whose only hope is that his client will not return with a complaint.

During the time of their exile in Babylon, the Israelites

felt abandoned by God. They had been deprived of their homeland and led off into slavery. It was a difficult, discouraging period for them, and with one voice the people cried out, "The Lord has forsaken me; my Lord has forgotten me." God sent his prophet to protest that it was not so. In a beautiful image God replied to the people through his prophet, "Can a mother forget her infant, be without tenderness for the child of her womb? Even should she forget, I will never forget you."

There are times, perhaps even many times, when we are tempted to wonder whether God really cares about us. When someone we love very much dies, especially when least expected, we may question why it had to be. We are often in the dark as to reasons why other misfortunes come upon us. Sometimes nothing seems to make sense any more. But we must never think that God is unconcerned or that he has abandoned us, even if everybody else has abandoned us. The test of real faith comes not in good times, but in bad ones. It is then that we must cling to the belief that our God cares.

THURSDAY OF THE FOURTH WEEK

Exodus 32, 7-14

> The whole episode of the golden calf, though it may refer to an earlier cultic apostasy even at Sinai, is primarily a condemnation of Jeroboam who set up the northern shrines of Dan and Bethel as cult centers in opposition to Jerusalem (cf. 1 K 12, 26 ff). Here God informs Moses of what the people have done. Notice that God does not speak of the people as "my people," but as "your people." The Lord has divorced himself from the people because of their sin. He is about to destroy them and make a new people for himself. But Moses intercedes for the people and persuades God to retract his decision. The motives Moses presents are God's reputation before the Egyptians and the promises he has made to the Patriarchs.

John 5, 31-47

> Jesus accepts the legal principle that a man is not to be believed on his own word. The application is to what he has just said: that the Son gives life and judges (5, 17-30). Therefore, Jesus calls forth his four witnesses. All of these are only four different aspects of the witness of "Another," i.e., the Father. (1) John the Baptist: The Jews had admitted that John was from God and he had witnessed to Jesus. (2) Jesus' miracles: They show he is from God for they could only have been given to him by the Father. (3) The Father himself: He speaks from within to those who believe but because they have never believed they have never heard this interior testimony. (4) The scriptures which come from God and point to Christ. Still, the Jews refuse to believe so as to have life. The basis of their disbelief is their refusal to dedicate themselves to God, to love him, and to seek his glory.

Reflection

In today's lesson we have witnessed an extraordinary scene: Moses standing before the irate God to intercede for the rebellious and ungrateful Israelites. God was angry with them because they had made a molten calf and worshipped it as God. He was so angry in fact that in speaking to Moses he referred to them not as "my people," but as "your people." He had divorced himself from the Israelites and was determined to destroy them and make a new people for himself. How fortunate they were to have Moses as their mediator before God because at his intercession God "relented in the punishment he had intended to inflict on his people."

Someone even greater than Moses is here as our mediator before God, the one about whom Moses wrote, Jesus Christ himself. As we saw earlier in Lent, Jesus taught us *how* to pray, but more than that he prayed *for* us and continues to pray for us and *with* us, especially in the Mass. It is true that we must humble ourselves before God and admit our weakness and our unworthiness as we do in the penitential rite of the Mass; however, we do not have to fear that God will reject our prayers or spurn our worship. We do not pray or worship alone or by our own power. We do so in union with Jesus.

Jesus, as it were, like a new Moses stands before his Father and says, "Why, O Lord, should your wrath blaze up against these people whom I have saved in my own blood. These are my people, for I have redeemed them, and therefore they are your people too." What we do today has value in the eyes of God because as he looks down upon us gathered for Mass he sees in us the person of his Son, our mediator, and he says: "This is my beloved Son in whom I am well pleased."

We should try to be especially conscious of our union with Jesus at the time of the consecration, when Jesus renews his sacrifice, and at the time when the solemn words of the great doxology are pronounced: "Through him, with him, in him, in the unity of the Holy Spirit, all glory and honor is yours, almighty Father, for ever and ever." To these words add your sincere and fervent "Amen" with the confidence that our worship is pleasing to the Father because Jesus is with us.

Alternate Reflection

Have you ever wondered why you have the faith? It is a good question to think about. Maybe you were born of parents who passed the faith on to you, but you could have been born of parents who had no religion. Maybe you are a convert, but you could have lived in a country in which people do not even hear the mention of Jesus Christ. Still another question is why have you kept the faith and not changed your mind about it.

The Israelites were a people especially favored by God. They received the gift of faith through God's revelation to them, and experienced his salvation in the exodus. And yet "they forgot the God who had saved them." Incredibly they abandoned the true God; they "made a calf in Horeb and adored a molten image." Why should we be more faithful than they?

When Jesus came, his credentials were overwhelming: his good works done in the Father's name, his miracles, and the very testimony of scripture itself. And yet the leaders of the people failed to respond to Jesus. Why is it that we accept Jesus whereas those men did not?

I think we have all met people who are obviously very good people. We feel that they are much more worthy than we to enjoy the gift of faith, and yet it is we who have the gift and not they. Why is it so?

The gift of faith is indeed a deep mystery, one which theologians have struggled to understand for centuries, but without much agreement among themselves. One thing is certain: we should be grateful for our faith, not with a smug complacency that we are better than others, but with a sincere humility which recognizes that faith is God's gift of which we are unworthy.

FRIDAY OF THE FOURTH WEEK

Wisdom 2, 1a, 12-22

God made man to be immortal. It was the wicked who invited death (spiritual death is meant: eternal separation from God) by their evil deeds. In 2, 1-20, the wicked man's outlook on life is presented by means of a speech. They deny any existence after death (1-5) and resolve to seek only their own pleasure in this life and to make strength the norm of justice (6-11). Since the life and words of the just man are a reproach to them, and because he will have nothing to do with them, the wicked decide to persecute him and test his belief that God will defend and take care of him in time of trouble (12-16). A judgment on these thoughts of the wicked follows (21-24). They are wrong in thinking that death has always been the inescapable fate of man. Because of their wickedness they did not know that God had made man to be immortal and that death comes only through sin.

John 7, 1-2, 10, 25-30

Having gone up to the feast in secret Jesus began to teach in the temple precincts and soon was involved in heated discussions with the Jews. Those aware of a plot to kill Jesus were surprised that he was being allowed to speak openly. It could not be that the authorities recognized him as the Messiah for everyone knew where he was from. The point here is that it was believed by some that when the Messiah came his origins would be unknown. But everyone knew that Jesus was from Nazareth and therefore he could not be the Messiah. The reply of Jesus was that their knowledge was superficial and they were unable to recognize his real origin, i.e., from the Father, because they did not know God. If they really knew God they would know that he is true and accept his testimony (cf. 5, 31-47). Jesus knows the Father in a unique way because the Father has sent him. This claim to divine origins resulted in an attempt to arrest him that failed.

Reflection

In the science fiction stories which appear occasionally on television, the theme generally runs about the same. Some unusual creature appears from outer space. The earthlings, without any investigation, react with fear and their first thought is to kill the creature. Almost instinctively, though irrationally, they feel that his death is necessary for their safety.

The reaction of many to Jesus was even more irrational.

Though it is true that Jesus, in a certain sense, came from outer space, he should have been recognized by the people as the Messiah because of his many signs and miracles. Far from being a threat to their safety, he came to be their salvation and to give them eternal life. And yet the leaders of the people plotted to kill Jesus. They felt that his death was necessary for their safety.

Perhaps the real reason for their plot can be found in the words of the wicked quoted in today's first lesson: "His life is not like other men's, and different are his ways. He judges us debased; he holds aloof from our paths as from things impure." Jesus was a living reproach to the leaders in their wickedness. And so they judged that the best thing to do was to kill him; that would get him out of the way for good. But "they knew not the hidden counsels of God nor did they count on a recompense of holiness." Death was not the end of Jesus, but only his gateway to eternal life and exaltation by his heavenly Father.

With Jesus we too must be bold enough to be different from the wicked; we must hold aloof from things that are impure. And we must face the consequences. There is enough evil in this world to make us suffer for trying to be good. Some may ridicule us as being odd, like some creature from outer space. But, as with Jesus, not even death will be our defeat, but only a gateway to eternal life and exaltation by our heavenly Father.

Alternate Reflection

Perhaps on first hearing you missed the full impact of one sentence in today's gospel: "They were looking for a chance to kill him." How chilling are those words; thinking about their meaning can make our blood run cold. They were looking for a chance to kill the very person who had come to save them from eternal death. And they had their foolish wish fulfilled when they saw Jesus dead on the cross.

Equally chilling are the words of the Epistle to the Hebrews in referring to those who have abandoned their faith: "They crucify again for themselves the Son of God and make him a mockery" (Heb 6, 6). Though these words were written as a vivid picture of the malice of apostasy, they can be applied without exaggeration to the evil of any deliberate mortal sin.

A lot of people these days do not like to hear this kind of talk about mortal sin from the pulpit. Many of us priests are slow to speak about serious sin lest we seem negative or old-fashioned. It is true that sometimes in the past there was too much emphasis on sin, fear, judgment, and hell and not enough on virtue, love, mercy, and heaven. But sin is not imaginary. It is real and a distinct possibility in our lives. Many of the readings during this season of Lent warn about the danger of complacency in religion. It is like the person who has been feeling fine only to discover that all along he has had a lurking tumor which has exploded into cancer. Perhaps if he had not been complacent about his health, if he had taken the trouble to get a thorough examination, the tumor could have been discovered in time.

We hope that at this moment we are spiritually healthy. Now is the time to search out even the smallest tumor of venial sin to destroy it. Now is the time to build up our spiritual health against a sudden attack. Now is the time to do everything we can, without complacency, to make sure that one day we are not so foolish as "to crucify again for ourselves the Son of God and make him a mockery."

SATURDAY OF THE FOURTH WEEK

Jeremiah 11, 18-20

Part of the first of the "Confessions" of Jeremiah in which he lays bare his soul, telling of his trials and sufferings. In the immediately preceding section Jeremiah was commanded by the Lord to tell the people that disaster was going to come upon them from which he would not save them because of their infidelity to the covenant. Then follows this account of how Jeremiah's relatives and fellow townsmen had planned to kill him. The exact circumstances or time of this plot are not known. Perhaps it was brought in here to show that preaching of the sort found in 11, 1-17, brought persecution upon Jeremiah. The text indicates that Jeremiah was almost caught unawares until he was informed about the plot by the Lord. Like a good Semite he places his cause before the Lord and asks for vengeance.

John 7, 40-53

In 7, 37-39, Jesus spoke of himself as the source of living water (cf. 4, 5-42). The reactions of the people is twofold: some identify Jesus as the Prophet-like-Moses who was to come at the time of the Messiah; others as the Messiah. But an objection is raised to his being the Messiah. It was believed by some that the Messiah would have to come from the Davidic city of Bethlehem. But the people thought that Jesus was born in Nazareth (John presupposes knowledge of the birth of Jesus in Bethlehem). Therefore, he could not be the Messiah. The Pharisees are upset by the following Jesus has found among the crowds and by the failure of the officers to arrest Jesus. Yet, one thing they are sure of is that no Pharisee has believed in him. But Nicodemus has believed and now rises to his defense, insisting on a point of law. He is sarcastically dismissed, for everyone knows that the eschatological prophet can not come from Galilee.

Reflection

Nicodemus was a Pharisee, a rabbi, and a member of the Sanhedrin, the high court which formed the supreme governing body of the Jews. His first meeting with Jesus (Jn

3, 1 ff), some time before the event of today's gospel, was a secret one at night because he was afraid of having his reputation tainted with his associates, all of whom vehemently opposed Jesus. On this occasion, however, he mustered enough courage to bring up a point of law in Jesus' favor. After the crucifixion, with still more courage, he assisted in the burial of Jesus (Jn 19, 39).

Our Lord looked for men who would have at least the courage of their convictions as did Nicodemus, but he found few. How disappointed he must have been to hear some out of cowardice bring up specious arguments against him from scripture itself. How saddened he must have been to see others intimidated by the Pharisees. Jeremiah, in the first reading, was a man of tremendous courage, and though he knew he was like a lamb being led to slaughter, he stuck to his convictions.

Like Nicodemus and even more like Jeremiah, we must have the courage of our convictions. We must be witnesses for Christ before others. Our religion is not fulfilled only by prayer and worship, for the Church is, as the Vatican Council expressed it, "the Church in the Modern World." It is especially your office as lay people to bring Christ to modern men. The *Decree on the Laity* says that you do this by "the very testimony of your Christian life and good works done in a supernatural spirit," but it points out also that "a true apostle looks for opportunities to announce Christ by words addressed either to non-believers with a view of leading them to faith, or to believers with a view to instructing and strengthening them and motivating them toward a more fervent life" (6).

Neither fear for our reputation or for our security is an excuse for failing to defend and proclaim Christ. Jesus wants, and needs, Catholics who have the courage of their convictions.

Alternate Reflection

You have noticed that when a man is arrested, reporters are careful to state that it is *alleged* that the man did so and so. The word, "alleged," or something similar is always used to avoid a statement indicating guilt before the case is tried in court. Moreover, when people are being selected for a jury every effort is made to choose people who have no prejudice in the case. The reason for all this is that in our system of justice a man is presumed innocent until he has been proven guilty before a jury of his peers.

Nicodemus tried to make the same point with the Pharisees who had already condemned Jesus. "Since when," he protested, "does our law condemn any man without first hearing him and knowing the facts?" The Pharisees had rejected Jesus without even an attempt to investigate the facts. They protested that the Messiah-Prophet would not come from Galilee but from Bethlehem. With but little trouble on their part they could have discovered that, though Jesus grew up in Nazareth in Galilee, he was indeed born in Bethlehem. The Pharisees were guilty of rash judgment.

Rash judgment is coming to a conclusion before all the facts are known. Unfortunately it is a fault that even good people can fall into. We hear a rumor about someone and we accept it as truth. Maybe we notice that someone is not going to communion and we judge that he or she must be guilty of mortal sin. Perhaps we see a man having lunch with a woman who is not his wife, and we conclude that they are having an affair. If we think that the rash judgment of the Pharisees against Jesus was a terrible crime, we had better think twice before passing judgment on anyone. In all these matters and ones like them a person should be innocent in our eyes until he has been judged guilty, not by a jury, but by the all knowing and just judge, God himself.

OPTIONAL MASS FOR THE FIFTH WEEK

2 Kings 4, 18b-21, 32-37

This is one of the miracle stories told about Elisha in 2 K 4, 1-8, 15. What is fact and what is fancy in these stories is hard to say. They are a part of the larger Elisha Cycle. The primary purpose of all these stories is to establish the authority of the prophets and focus attention on the fulfillment of the prophetic word. The full impact of this particular story is understood only when one remembers that the child was born in the woman's old age as a result of a prophecy of Elisha (4, 8-17). The child seemingly died of a sunstroke.

John 11, 1-45

This is the seventh and last of Jesus' "signs" which point to him as the life-giver. The physical life given to Lazarus is meant to be a sign of the power of Jesus to grant eternal life here on earth and a promise that on the last day he will raise the dead. The whole is a dramatization of the doctrine contained in vv. 25-27. In response to Martha's profession of faith in the final resurrection (24) Jesus says: "I am the resurrection and the life." He affirms her belief in the final resurrection and points out to her that he is the source of that resurrection and life here and now. Verses 25-26 are a further comment on this statement. He is the resurrection in the sense that whoever believes in him, though he shall die physically, shall arrive at eternal life. He is the life in that whoever has life through belief in him will never die a spiritual death for the life he gives now is eternal life.

Reflection

The two awesome realities with which all humans must

be concerned are life and death. We fear death and cling to life. We do everything we can to put off the moment of death, and we yearn for a good life that will never end.

In times past men searched for the fountain of youth so that they might always be young and might never have to die. Today scientists are probing into the aging process in the hope of finding a way to prolong life and eventually prevent death. Such searching and probing miss the point. The life for which we are made is not found in this world, but in heaven, and to find it we must, like Christ, pass through death to a sharing in his resurrection.

Jesus is the key to eternal life. He tells us today: "I am the resurrection and the life: whoever believes in me, though he should die, will come to life." The tremendous miracle related in today's gospel was not only an act of compassion, but also a sign of Christ's power over life and death. Jesus has the power to overcome death and to grant eternal life to those who are faithful to him.

We do not have to fear a physical aging process that will lead to death; we need only fear the disruptive power of sin which alone can destroy us. There is no fountain of youth except Jesus himself, who said, "The water I give shall become a fountain, leaping up to provide eternal life." Whoever believes in Jesus, though he should die, will come to life.

MONDAY OF THE FIFTH WEEK

Daniel 13, 1-9, 15-17, 19-30, 33-62 (short form: 41c-62)
    The story of the chaste Susanna comes from a collection of folk tales about a legendary Daniel that circulated, in the late pre-Christian era, independently of the book of Daniel. This story

about Susanna, as also the one about Bel and the Dragon, is a later addition to the book of Daniel. The story of Susanna is easily followed. The difficulty is in stating the purpose of the story. The most obvious purpose would be to show that, with God's help, virtue will triumph over vice; God will save those who remain faithful to him. Some exegetes seek deeper meanings in the story (see commentaries). There may be such but there is no real agreement on what these deeper meanings are.

John 8, 1-11 (A and B cycle)

This story is a later addition to the gospel of John and probably is not Johannine in origin. The purpose of the scribes and Pharisees is to trap Jesus. But exactly what Jesus is being asked to give a decision on is not clear. Still, the point of the story is clear. Jesus is here shown as a judge who extends mercy to the sinner in order to turn the sinner from his sin. There is no idea here of indifference to sin on the part of Jesus. He is simply asking the accusers to examine their own consciences before carrying out the judgment. It is clear to Jesus that they are using the woman simply to trap him and have no concern for her state of soul. Jesus does. They withdraw in embarrassment.

John 8, 12-20 (C cycle)

A theme of the feast of Booths (the general context) was that of light which symbolized the divine presence. Here Jesus proclaims that he is the light of the world, the divine presence among men for in him one finds the revelation of God which makes known to man the purpose and meaning of life. The Pharisees seek verification of this. Jesus insists that his testimony is true because he knows where he comes from and they do not. He also gives two witnesses: Himself and his Father. When they ask Jesus to produce the Father he tells them that if they really recognized and accepted him they would know the Father. In the midst of this discussion (15-16) he says that he judges no one but that his presence among men causes them to judge themselves by their rejection or acceptance of him. This judgment is valid and will be ratified at the final judgment by himself and the Father (cf. 5, 17-30).

Reflection (A & B Cycle)

It is true that the law of Moses stated that the penalty for adultery was death. The scribes and the Pharisees in today's gospel, however, seemed to enjoy the misery of the poor woman as they dragged her before Jesus. They were perverse in that they hoped to use her sad condition in order to trap Jesus. But our Lord would neither be trapped nor be a partner to their gloating self-righteousness.

It is not that our Lord condoned the sin of adultery or pretended that it was not evil. Rather Jesus revealed that he is a judge who extends mercy to the sinner in order to turn him away from sin. Our Lord knew what was in the woman's heart, and it must have been that he saw there the spark of repentance, which won his forgiveness. He told her to avoid the sin in the future as a sign of her repentance.

Susanna, in contrast to this woman, was falsely accused of adultery. Until Daniel appeared on the scene, all the people believed her guilty and condemned her to death. In her innocence she had trusted in God, and her trust was rewarded by acquittal.

Sometimes we are rightly accused by others because we do make mistakes; we do commit sins. Some people may even seem to enjoy our misery at the time. We must remember, however, that Jesus is the judge who wishes to extend mercy to us, no matter what others may think about us, provided we show the spark of repentance. On the other hand, we are sometimes falsely accused, and in one way that can be an even more painful situation. It is then that we must turn to God, like Susanna, and put our trust in his power to vindicate us. In either case, it is how we stand in the sight of God that really counts.

Reflection (C Cycle)

Susanna, the wife of Joakim, was falsely accused of adultery by the two elders. How distressful it must have been for Susanna in her innocence to see herself being condemned, while the two elders in their guilt were going free. Indeed it looked as if the elders would have their day until Daniel appeared on the scene. Face to face with Daniel, and caught by his shrewdness, they condemned themselves. In much the same way, the Pharisees, who wished to accuse Jesus of blasphemy and deceit, face to face with Jesus manifested their own sinfulness by their rejection of him. Jesus had just said that he was the light of the world, and it was his penetrating light which revealed their wickedness.

Sometimes we may be tempted to be distressed about people who seem to be "getting way with murder." Maybe we feel spiteful toward them, or perhaps a little envious. We work hard, try to be good and to do the right thing all the time, while others who seem to have little care for God or anyone but themselves prosper and have everything their own way. We may think that we are better off than they morally, and yet they are better off than we financially, socially, and in every other material way. What happens to such people is God's concern. We should not wish evil for them, but as a matter of fact if they are guilty of sin they will be judged by God and receive his condemnation as did the two elders.

Actually we should be concerned with how we stand before God, without making any comparison of ourselves with others. Such comparison not only can lead to self deception, but misses the point. We are what we are before God, and we will be judged, not in contrast with our fellow human beings, but in the light of the holiness of Christ.

TUESDAY OF THE FIFTH WEEK

Numbers 21, 4-9

Trying to enter directly into Palestine from the South, at the end of their stay in the desert, the Israelites found the way blocked and they had to skirt Edom so as to come in from the East. The people were not happy about the detour and began to grumble against God and Moses. As a punishment the Lord sent poisonous snakes among the people and many died. They then admitted that they had sinned by their grumbling and lack of faith in God and asked Moses to intercede for them with the Lord. Moses was told to make a bronze serpent, erect it as a standard, and whoever looked on it would be healed. This looks like magic but the author emphasizes that it is the Lord who controls the whole situation and who heals. What is demanded of the people when they are told to look on the standard is faith in God's power. John will see this erecting of the bronze serpent as a type of Christ's crucifixion (Jn 3, 14-16).

John 8, 21-30

Jesus informs the Jews what their rejection of him means. He is soon to return to the Father and they will die without the gift of eternal life because of their rejection of him. Misunderstanding him the Jews speak a profound truth. He will voluntarily lay down his life and because they have rejected him they will loose eternal life. He has come from heaven to give them the life that the world is incapable of giving. They can acquire this life only by believing that he bears the divine name "I Am." Still misunderstanding they ask who he is. His answer: the unique representative of the Father as he has always claimed. He only speaks the words of the Father which are truthful and bring their own condemnation on those who reject them. Still they misunderstand. He tells them that after his death and his glorification it will be clear to them who he is: the bearer of the divine name who comes from the Father, who is always with him.

Reflection

We have all heard about parents who have disowned their child. It may have been because of a marriage the parents did not approve, or because the son or daughter has gone off to live a hippie-type existence. Whatever the reason, it is a terrible thing to hear a father or mother say, "Out of my sight! You are no child of mine!"

So-called fire and brimstone sermons are no longer popular. Nor would such a sermon be appropriate for you. However, it is healthy sometimes to remember that it would be a very terrible thing for any of us to hear from God, "Out of my sight! You are no child of mine!" After all, the Church in this Mass has had us listen to the words of Jesus, "You will surely die in your sins unless you come to believe that I am." If we do not wish to die in our sins, we must turn to Christ as our savior. When the Israelites in the desert were punished for their sins by means of deadly serpents, they were saved by turning in faith toward the bronze serpent lifted up by Moses. St. John the evangelist saw in the lifting up of the serpent a type or sign of Jesus' being lifted up on the cross, and he wrote, "Just as Moses lifted up the serpent in the desert, so must the Son of Man be lifted up, that all who believe may have eternal life in him" (Jn 3, 14).

And so we turn to Christ in faith because we want to have eternal life. We want no part of mortal sin, but as God's children we should be concerned about even small offenses against God. Small sins count too. It is good for all of us to remember that we should take venial sins seriously, in the sense that we should really be trying to please God in all things. Jesus lifted up on the cross has the power to save us not only from the deadly bite of mortal sin but also from the minor prick of venial sin.

Alternate Reflection

Jesus told the Pharisees that where he was going they

could not come. Somehow they foolishly interpreted his words to mean that Jesus was going to commit suicide, and consequently go to hell where they as "righteous" men could not follow. It was a case of supreme irony. As a matter of fact Jesus would lay down his life, not in suicide but in sacrifice, and he would thereby pass, not to hell, but to the glory of heaven where indeed the self-righteous Pharisees could not go because of their sins.

The gospels show that Jesus had come to call sinners out of love for them. He was considerate of the tax collectors, lenient toward the woman taken in adultery, and merciful toward those suffering because of their sins. Yet Jesus was stern with the Pharisees, and to no one else did he address such words as, "You will die in your sins; where I am going you cannot come."

The Pharisees had taken the heart and spirit out of religion. They thought their salvation was guaranteed because of their descent from Abraham, and they had reduced religion to nothing more than a hypocritical observance of a multiplicity of minute regulations. They were complacent; they thought they had it made. In their smugness they had placed themselves out of the reach of Jesus, and in their self-sufficiency they believed that they did not need the help of Jesus or anyone else.

Complacency is deadly, whatever be its cause. St. Paul (Phil 2, 12) says that we must work out our salvation in fear—not the fear of God but the fear of ourselves for we are weak and without Jesus we can do nothing (Jn 15, 5).

WEDNESDAY OF THE FIFTH WEEK

Daniel 3, 14-20, 91-92, 95

The three Hebrew youths refused to worship the golden statue that the king had set up. In the face of his threats to throw them into the furnace, if they did not comply, they confessed their belief that their God, Yahweh, could save them, if he wished, but whether he did or not they still refused to worship the idol. Therefore, they are thrown into the furnace but are delivered by an angel sent by God. The king is highly impressed that their God has intervened to save those who were ready to die rather than worship another god. The point of the story is clear enough: the God of Israel will protect his people from harm if they remain faithful to him. The lesson of the story was quite pertinent for the Jews in Palestine around 165 B.C. when Antiochus IV was ordering the Jews to take part in pagan worship under the threat of death.

John 8, 31-42

Behind this discourse is the Jewish belief that being a descendant of Abraham is an automatic guarantee of salvation. Jesus tells the people what is necessary to be his disciple: to not only hear his word but to live according to it constantly. If they do this, they will possess the truth, the revelation of Jesus, and this will free them from sin. As descendants of Abraham they insist that they are already free. Jesus responds that simply being a Jew does not make one free, for everyone who sins is a slave of sin. They can be freed from sin only through the Son. They may be descendants of Abraham but they do not act like it for they do not accept and act according to the word which he has received from the Father. The Jews insist Abraham is their Father. But Jesus replies that their works show them not to be real children of Abraham but children of the devil. This they deny. Jesus responds that if they were children of God they would recognize that he is from God.

Reflection

A growing problem in our society is that of drug abuse. Those drugs which are addictive, after giving temporary satisfaction, leave the user with a driving need for more and more. The addict loses his freedom; he becomes a slave of dope. If he finds no cure, he eventually becomes a dropout from his family, from society, from everything.

One can also become a slave of sin. Any sin gives only a temporary satisfaction. Unless one turns immediately back to God, sin leaves a person with a driving need for more and more in a blind, desperate search for happiness. Jesus said in the gospel today: "Everyone who lives in sin is the slave of sin." Jesus came to set us free from the slavery of sin. The Jews who heard the words of Jesus were insulted by his implying that they were slaves. They protested that they were free because they were sons of Abraham, and they thereby betrayed their mistaken belief that being a descendant of Abraham was an automatic guarantee of salvation. Jesus indicated that such physical descent was not enough, and that because of their evil works they were really slaves after all, and as slaves they had in effect become dropouts from the household of God.

The lesson for us is obvious. We are sons of God by our baptism, but just being a Catholic is no automatic guarantee of salvation. We too, amid all the confusing enticements and mixed up values of our society, run the risk of becoming slaves of sin. It is never a sudden process, just as the slavery of dope addiction is never a sudden process. Little by little small sins can get a hold on us until a serious sin becomes easy. Then one sin leads to another until we are enslaved. We cannot afford the luxury of complacency. With the grace of God we must constantly guard and nourish the filial love for God in our hearts lest, as slaves to sin, we become drop-outs from the family of God.

Alternate Reflection

On July 10, 1970 Communist China released Bishop James Walsh from prison, reportedly because of advanced age and ill health. The bishop had been arrested in 1958 and held incommunicado for almost two years before he was sentenced to twenty years in prison on charges of spying for the United States and the Vatican. When his brother was allowed to visit him in 1960, the bishop told him, "While no one likes to be confined, I am not unhappy here and I leave the future entirely in the hands of God." He had found that "four walls do not a prison make, nor iron bars a cage."

During those long years in a small cell of a prison on the outskirts of Shanghai, Bishop Walsh did not enjoy freedom in the ordinary sense, but he did learn the meaning of the words of Jesus, "If you live according to my teaching, you are truly my disciples; then you will know the truth and the truth will set you free."

Jesus taught that cells and prisons do not destroy free-dom; sin does that. Sin makes us slaves. It chains the human spirit and restricts us from living in such a way as to achieve the real happiness for which we all yearn. Freedom is the liberty not to do whatever we want, but to do whatever we must in order to fulfill our spiritual destiny. Living a life of sin is like choosing to confine oneself within a run-down, one room hovel and pretending that is pleasure, when one could live in a magnificent mansion forever.

If we live according to the teaching of Jesus as his disci-ples, his truth will set us free—free from sin with the liberty to pursue the true purpose of life.

THURSDAY OF THE FIFTH WEEK

Genesis 17, 3-9

The Priestly tradition's version of God's covenant with Abraham. All the attention is placed on God as the principal actor. Abraham simply listens and makes a sign of reverence. God is the only one bound by this covenant. In vv. 9-14 circumcision is imposed on Abraham and his descendants but it is only a sign of the covenant and not a covenant obligation. God binds himself to three things: to give Abram numerous descendants; to give Abram and his descendants the land to which they have recently immigrated; to be their God. Closely linked to the promise of numerous prosperity is the change of Abram's name to Abraham. This emphasizes that a new era is about to begin with the covenant. The meaning of the name also explains Abraham's destiny: to be the "father of a multitude." Finally, it is pointed out that this covenant is being made not only with Abraham but with all his descendants—it is to be a "perpetual covenant" valid for all times.

John 8, 51-59

Jesus has accused the Jews of being children of Satan (8, 41-47). They claim that he is possessed. He denies this and warns them that God will judge them for what they have said about him (48-50). But if they will keep his word, hear it and obey it, they can have eternal life. They misunderstand him and think he means deliverance from physical death. At this they scoff. Is he greater than Abraham and the prophets who died! Jesus insists that he is not seeking glory for himself by his claims. His Father, who is their God, will vindicate him by glorifying him. He knows the Father and obeys him while they lie in saying that they know him. Yes, he is greater than Abraham who was but his forerunner and who had a vision of him (Gn 17, 17) and rejoiced. At this the Jews also scoff, not understanding him. In answer Jesus emphatically proclaims his divine name, "I am." The Jews understand his claim and move to stone him but he escapes.

Reflection

A smalltime, virtually unknown politician in a campaign speech boasts that he is a better man than George Washington. What is the reaction of the crowd? Some are indignant at his presumption. Others simply reject him as a fool. Still others are so enraged that they want to run him out of town.

Jesus in today's gospel was not giving a campaign speech, for he was not running for election. He had been chosen and sent by God. But his claim to be greater than Abraham was, in the estimation of the Jews, even wilder than the politician's boast of being greater than George Washington, the father of our country. Abraham was indeed the father of the Jews, as well as of all the Semitic peoples, a man of faith, devotion, and courage. And yet the claim of Jesus to be greater than Abraham was no vain boast. The Jews may have thought of him as small town stuff, but he emphatically states that he is divine by declaring, "Before Abraham came to be, I AM." They may have looked upon him as virtually unknown, but Jesus was known and chosen by his Father to fulfill all of the covenant promises made to Abraham, who from heaven rejoiced to see Jesus coming into the world.

God promised Abraham, "I will maintain my covenant with you and your descendants after you throughout the ages as an everlasting pact, to be your God and the God of your descendants after you." Jesus came in fulfillment of this covenant, a greater fulfillment than even Abraham could ever have dreamed possible. We as Christians are the beneficiaries of that covenant and its fulfillment. How right and just it is for us to give thanks and praise to God in this Mass in which we renew our covenant with God in the blood of Jesus.

Alternate Reflection

Abraham, the father of the Israelites, was indeed a marvelous man. He had many virtues, such as courage, determination, and fortitude, but in today's lesson his greatest virtue is subtly manifested: his docile faith. God made astounding promises to this simple nomad, but Abraham did not say, "How can you do all these things?" or "What proof do you offer of your truth and your power?" He simply listened in reverent silence and accepted God's word on its face value, without confirming miracles or signs on God's part.

In contrast the Jews of today's gospel did nothing but oppose the teaching of Jesus. Scarcely had Jesus gotten the words out of his mouth when they were protesting and objecting to everything he had said. And they had plenty of reason at least to listen patiently to Jesus because of all the signs and wonders he had done to support his claims. For whatever reason, they did not have docile faith.

Some people say that faith is blind, but faith is no more blind than love is. Love sees through appearances to the true worth and beauty of a person which others, with but a superficial glance, easily miss. True love sharpens visions, and docile faith does the same. Our faith should make us see through the maze of confusion and conflict through which our lives are passing to the final goal of happiness toward which the loving hand of God is directing us. Our faith should make us see through the frustration and turmoil of our present existence to the life of fulfillment which God has promised us.

God is patient. He took centuries to prepare the world for the coming of the Messiah in accord with the promises made to the docile Abraham. The saving work of Jesus continues in our world and will not be completed until the final coming of Jesus, a coming toward which we must look with docile faith.

FRIDAY OF THE FIFTH WEEK

Jeremiah 20, 10-13

In ch. 19 Jeremiah foretells the destruction of Jerusalem. He is arrested, beaten, and put in the stocks overnight (20, 1-6). After this episode an editor has inserted one of the "Confessions" of Jeremiah (20, 7-18) to show the suffering this caused him. Jeremiah strongly complains to the Lord about the derision and abuse and the internal suffering that the prophetic office has brought him (7-9). But even in the midst of his suffering he can and does put his trust in God (10-11). The source of his confidence is Yahweh's promise that he would always be with Jeremiah and that his enemies would not overcome him (1, 8, 19). Jeremiah is sure of Yahweh's loyalty to his promise. Verse 13 is a call to praise the Lord who takes care of those who are poor, i.e., pious, trusting.

John 10, 31-42

In the Temple precincts, during the feast of the dedication, Jesus is asked if he is the Messiah. He insists on his unity with the Father (10, 22-30). The Jews understand that he is claiming equality with God and want to kill him. He recalls to them his works which obviously come from God. They insist it is not for his works but for his blasphemy, his claim to be God, that they wish to stone him. Jesus responds with a typical rabbinical argument. In the Old Testament (Ps 82, 6) the judges could be called gods because they were vehicles of God's word. **A fortiori** Jesus can all the more be called God since he has been consecrated and sent into the world as a unique vehicle of the word of God. Therefore, there is no blasphemy. That he is the unique vehicle of the word of God is clear from his works which also reveal his unity with the Father and hence his divine origin. Again he escapes from their attempt to arrest him.

Reflection

One of the most amazing things in the life of Jesus is the fact that so many people rejected him. Jesus is the personification of all that is good and holy and desirable, and he wishes to draw all men to himself to make them perfectly and eternally happy. Not only did he preach the goodness and love of his Father for men, but he himself revealed that goodness and love by his actions. When some wanted to stone him, he protested, "Many good deeds have I shown you from the Father. For which of these do you stone me?" They then accused him of blasphemy because he made himself God, and yet he was but speaking the truth, and his claim to be divine was confirmed by signs and miracles.

The rejection that Jesus suffered was nothing new. Jeremiah, who did nothing but speak the truth in God's name, was likewise rejected (first reading). When he warned the people about the destruction of Jerusalem unless they repented, he was arrested, beaten, and put in stocks.

Yes, it is amazing that Jesus, as well as Jeremiah and other prophets in Israel, were rejected by so many people when they spoke the truth. Why were they rejected? There are many complicated reasons, but one reason is that sometimes the truth can hurt. When the truth makes us face our own failures and inadequacies, the easiest way to escape our responsibilities and the need to change is to ignore or deny the truth. When a teacher informs irresponsible parents that their child is both a scholastic and a disciplinary problem in school, that evaluation is a judgment of the parents as well as the child. Rather than face their own failure and the need to do something about the child, the parents take the easy way out and refuse to accept the teacher's report.

The truth can hurt, even the truth preached by Jesus. The truth of Jesus demands that we be different from others, it requires that we accept suffering and self-denial, and that we abandon our selfishness to be generous in our love and service of others. Let us pray in the Mass that we will never take the easy way out by rejecting Jesus and his truth.

Alternate Reflection

When Jesus was on this earth, his humanity was a stumbling block for his enemies. It was shocking to them that this former carpenter, who hailed from the inconspicuous town of Nazareth, laid claim to divinity. The leaders of the people, infuriated by his claim, accused him of blasphemy. "You who are only a man are making yourself God," they complained.

We look back upon Jesus through the eyes of faith. Because of our faith we are amazed that the people of the day were so blind to the divinity of Christ. It may even be that our faith in his divinity is so strong that we fail to appreciate the reality of his humanity. The leaders of the people were wrong in thinking of Jesus only as a man, falsely claiming to be God, but we are equally wrong if we think of him only as God, masquerading, as it were, in the costume of a human body. Jesus, though truly God, was just as human as we are in all things but sin.

During this coming week, Holy Week, we will meditate once more on the passion and death of Jesus. His pain and anguish during that ordeal were no fiction. When Jesus struggled with himself in the garden of Gethsemane to accept the chalice of suffering offered him by his Father, he experienced the same confusion that we ourselves have felt when face to face with a serious temptation. When Peter denied him and Judas betrayed him, he knew the same sadness we have known when a relative or friend has hurt us deeply. When the soldiers mocked him and spat on him, he was just as humiliated as we when we have been insulted or made little of. His pain in the crucifixion was true torture, and his agony was true torment.

Indeed it was God who suffered and died to save us from our sins, but he did so as a real human being.

SATURDAY OF THE FIFTH WEEK

Ezekiel 37, 21-28

Ezekiel describes for the exiles the new Israel that is to arise once God has completed his punishment of the people for their sins. The two kingdoms, Israel and Judah, will once again be joined to form a new kingdom under a new David. The Lord will cleanse the people of their sins and preserve them from any future apostasy. Under the new David they will live in obedience and faithfulness and occupy the land of their fathers forever. A new covenant will be established between God and the people, a covenant of peace which will be everlasting: Yahweh will be their God and they his people and above all else he will once again dwell in their midst. The presence of his sanctuary in their midst will be a sign of the renewed covenant and a sign to the nations that it is Yahweh who has sanctified his people and they will bow down before him.

John 11, 45-56

Jesus' gift of life to Lazarus (11, 1-44) now leads to his own death. Many who witnessed this miracle believe, but others report the incident to the Pharisees, and a meeting of the Sanhedrin is called. They must decide what to do, for many are believing in him. If he is some kind of revolutionary Rome may intervene and destroy the Temple and the nation. Caiaphas then makes the statement toward which all has been leading. His advice is pure political expediency: Get rid of Jesus lest he provoke the Romans to destroy the nation. The explanation which follows points out that he had unknowingly prophesied the truth: Jesus would die for the nation but not for the nation alone but for all men, to make them all one. From then on they planned to kill Jesus and so he withdrew. As the Passover draws near everyone is waiting to see if he will show up in Jerusalem since orders have been given for his arrest.

Reflection

God has given us the precious gift of freedom, and he respects that freedom. Some people abuse their freedom by doing evil, but God, rather than take freedom away, uses his wisdom to draw good from evil. This is an important lesson that we see in today's gospel.

The chief priests and the Pharisees were afraid that if the people were to follow Jesus, the Romans would come and take over their temple and their country. Caiaphas, the high priest, using his freedom of decision, told his companions that the simplest solution to the problem was to kill Jesus. He pointed out that it was better for this one man to die than for the whole nation to be destroyed. From that day on the leaders of the people plotted to kill Jesus.

What Caiaphas and the others did not realize was that God would draw good from their evil plan, and even from the words of Caiaphas. It was indeed better that Jesus die in sacrifice than the whole human race perish in sin. God the Father's plan was that the death of his son would atone for our sins. He allowed the leaders of the people to set in motion all the events that led to the death of Jesus because he knew that his son would accept death eagerly and willingly for the salvation of the world.

We are in a position to see how God worked good through the evil plot to kill Jesus. In our own lives at the present moment it is often difficult or even sometimes impossible to know just what God has in mind when he allows evil. But we must have the faith to believe that God knows what he is doing. His respect for freedom allows evil, but in his wisdom he knows how to draw good from evil and in his love he does so. Perhaps we think that if we were running the world we would do things differently. God's ways are not our ways, but his ways are best.

Alternate Reflection

Tomorrow we begin Holy Week, which at one time was referred to as "the great week." It is truly a great week because within it we will commemorate the events of our salvation. The liturgy, however, does not present the passion of our Lord in merely sad or sorrowful terms as if we did not know the outcome. There is no tragic note about the suffering and death of our Lord as if he were a failure, dragged down to defeat by the machinations of such men as Caiaphas and the Pharisees. Rather throughout the week there runs a feeling of joyful victory generated by the realization that the death of Jesus led to the glory of his resurrection.

We will begin the week tomorrow with the praise and glorification of Jesus as the Messiah-King in the procession of the palms. The shouts and cheers of the people of Palm Sunday are but a foreshadowing of the true glory bestowed upon Jesus by his heavenly Father in his resurrection on Easter Sunday. On Palm Sunday, after the triumphal procession, Jesus instructed his apostles in a veiled way concerning the mysterious events that were to follow. He said, "Unless the grain of wheat falls to the earth and dies, it remains just a grain of wheat; but if it dies, it produces much fruit" (Jn 12, 24 f). Jesus was that grain of wheat which had to die and be planted in the earth for three days. Then he would, as it were, push upward on Easter Sunday through earth like a growing stalk of wheat bearing much fruit. That fruit was his glorification and our salvation. His life has become our life and his glory, our glory.

During this coming week the liturgy will give us the opportunity to relive with Christ his paschal mystery. Let us pray that our union with him through this week may bear the fruit of eternal life.

MONDAY OF HOLY WEEK

Isaiah 42, 1-7

Verses 1-4 contain the first of the Servant Songs and present the investiture of the Servant by God. He is one who has been specially chosen by God and endowed with the spirit of God, the power of God, to accomplish a mission to all the nations. As a king and prophet his mission is to "bring forth justice," i.e., to reveal to the nations that Yahweh alone is God and so to bring salvation to them. He will carry out his mission quietly and patiently. Verses 5-7 (actually 5-9) are probably a commentary on the Son. God can do as he says because he is the creator of all. Here it is supposed that the servant is Israel (cf. 41, 9). She is to be the tool whereby God effects the salvation of the gentiles, bringing to them enlightenment and liberation from suffering.

John 12, 1-11

With the final Passover drawing near Jesus goes to Bethany. During a meal there Mary anoints his feet with some costly ointment and wipes them with her hair. Judas complains that the ointment should have been sold and the money given to the poor. John uses this opportunity to portray Judas as a thief and remarks that his complaint was hypocritical. Verse 7 explains the meaning of the anointing: it is an anointing of Jesus' body for burial, a preparation for his death. As with Caiaphas it is an unconscious prophecy of his death. Verses 9-11 form a transition to Jesus' entry into Jerusalem. The hatred of the Jewish leaders for Jesus even extends to Lazarus because many are believing in Jesus as a result of Lazarus' having been raised from the dead.

Reflection

In today's gospel St. John makes one of his few chronological references. He notes that the anointing took place "six days before Passover." That was the day on which the Jews were instructed to procure the lamb that would be used for the Passover meal and to keep it until the day before Passover when it was to be slaughtered during the evening twilight (Ex 12, 3). The Passover meal was a commemoration of the saving events of the exodus. The Israelites at the time of the exodus were told to sprinkle the blood of the lamb on the lintel and the two doorposts of their houses. Then at midnight the angel of God struck down all the first born of the Egyptians, but seeing the blood on the lintel and the two doorposts, he passed over the houses of the Israelites. They were saved because of the blood of the lamb.

It would seem that somehow in the mind of St. John the anointing of Jesus was his being selected and prepared to be the Christian paschal lamb. Indeed it is the blood of Christ that saves us from sin. Before communion you hear these words, "This is the lamb of God who takes away the sins of the world." As the true paschal lamb, Jesus is the fulfillment of all of those years of promise and preparation found in the Old Testament. For century after century God patiently directed his people toward the great events which we relive this week in the liturgy. We do not look to the future as did the Jews of old; rather we have the privilege of sharing directly and personally in the saving mysteries of Jesus, the lamb who takes away the sins of the world.

Alternate Reflection

Mary's anointing of Jesus was indeed an extravagance. Judas, a shrewd calculator of monetary worth, estimated that the perfume could have been sold for three hundred pieces of silver (perhaps ten month's wages, and incidentally ten times more than Jesus was worth in his eyes). Jesus saw in Mary's impetuous act a beautiful sign of love (cf. Mk 14, 6). Love does not always correspond with cold logic, and there is room in religion for deeds which spring more from the heart than from the intellect. It is true that the perfume could have been sold for the benefit of the poor, but Jesus, who took second place to no one in his concern for the poor, graciously accepted Mary's extravagance.

The protest of Judas was hypocritical, made from no concern for the poor, since his hope was to have pocketed the price of the perfume for himself. Today in the Church there has been a healthy renewal of concern for the poor, and in many respects we all need such a renewal. And yet some, though with a sincerity never felt by Judas, seem to be making of religion nothing but the service of the poor. No excuse should be manufactured for hoarded or abused wealth on the part of anyone in the Church; however, there is much more to religion than the alleviation of poverty, important though it be. Mary had learned that Jesus is the resurrection and the life, and her act was one of loving recognition. The wish to spend the money on the poor involved a lack of recognition of the real nature of Jesus as the Son of God. There must always be a time and a place for service of the poor, but there must also be a time and a place for the due worship of the person of the Son of God.

TUESDAY OF HOLY WEEK

Isaiah 49, 1-6

The second Servant Song. Here it is the Servant who speaks and addresses the nations. He tells them how he had been called by God and given his mission while still in the womb. God equipped him for this mission by endowing his word with power to penetrate and to range far and wide and by putting the Servant under his protection. At first his mission had been to Israel, to bring her back to God. But it had seemed to him that his work was in vain and he had been discouraged. From this he had learned to put his trust in God and not to seek a return from his work but only from God. But though his early work had seemed to him to be in vain it must have gained God's approval for the Lord has now given him a new task: to extend his mission of salvation to all the nations. (The Servant is here identified as Israel [v. 3]. Perhaps this is to be understood as the ideal Israel.)

John 13, 21-33, 36-38

At the Last Supper Jesus foretells his betrayal by Judas. The author brings out that even over this event Jesus has complete control for Judas does not leave to effect the betrayal until Jesus permits him to go. Jesus controls his own destiny. By mentioning that it was night when Judas left the author shows that the hour of darkness, the time of Jesus' death, has arrived. After the departure of Judas, Jesus tells his apostles that the time for his glorification, and that of the Father, has arrived since Judas has gone to get his captors who will put him to death. This glorification involves his returning to the Father and leaving them. But their inability to follow him is temporary for in time they will follow him through their own death and resurrection to life. Peter does not fully understand and professes complete loyalty. Jesus tells him that before the night is over he will deny him.

Reflection

Two men in the gospel are alike, and yet totally different. They are Simon Peter and Judas Iscariot. They are alike in that they both failed Jesus, Peter by denial and Judas by betrayal. They are totally different from each other in their reaction to Jesus after their failure; Peter repented and Judas despaired.

Peter's character was so human that I think all of us can feel very close to him. He was eager, yet weak; sincere, yet faltering; devoted, yet temporarily disloyal. Above all he knew Jesus so well that he was quick to repentance and confident of forgiveness.

We hope and pray that we will not end up as Judas did, but how like Peter most of us are. We are eager to form resolutions to do great things for Christ, but often we are remiss in carrying out those good resolutions. We are sincere in our zeal for Christ, but frequently we falter through human weakness. We are truly devoted to Christ, but sometimes we may live almost as if we did not know Christ and his teachings.

If we are like Peter in his faults, we should try to be like him also in his strong points. Peter came to know Jesus well. Because he knew Jesus well and had witnessed his love for sinners, Peter was confident of forgiveness. But what about Judas? We cannot afford to be like him in any way. Judas had the same opportunities to know Jesus that Peter had. He had heard his teaching and seen his example. He had been offered love by Jesus. But he squandered his opportunities to know Christ and he failed to respond to Jesus' offer of love.

During this Holy Week we have a valuable opportunity of knowing Jesus by meditating on the events of his passion and death. He suffered all that he had to endure out of love for us. Today let us pray for the grace to respond to love as Peter did.

Alternate Reflection

During the last hours of Jesus on this earth, St. Peter learned a bitter lesson: words are cheap. All you have to do is open your mouth and let them come out, but if they are not backed up by actions they are as worthless as counterfeit money or a bad check.

At the Last Supper poor Peter opened his mouth and let the words come out. He said to Jesus, "I will lay down my life for you." At the moment he did not realize that his words were counterfeit. It was only later, when he was challenged concerning his association with Jesus, that he realized how worthless those words were. While Jesus was standing trial before the high priest, a servant girl noticed Peter in the courtyard and accused him of being a follower of Jesus. And this man, who a few hours before had said that he would die for Jesus, said to the girl, "I don't know what you are talking about." A little later when some bystanders accused him of the same thing, he replied, "I don't even know the man you are talking about!" Then he heard the second cock crow and broke down and began to cry. It was a bitter lesson for Peter to learn.

But learn the lesson he did. Peter determined to make good his words at the Last Supper, not with a bad check, but with a blank check on which he would allow Jesus to fill in the amount he wished. And so it was that many years after the crucifixion Peter followed his master to a martyr's death on a cross.

If we are good Christians we will tell Jesus that we will follow him to death rather than deny him or be disloyal to him in any way, even in little things. In fact, we should write Jesus a blank check and allow him to require any amount from us. We must remember, however, that our payment cannot be counterfeit; it must be backed up with the silver and gold of sincerity and truth.

WEDNESDAY OF HOLY WEEK

Isaiah 50, 4-9a

The third Servant Song. In this song we have an act of confidence and trust in God made by the Servant. He described how he was open to the Lord, receiving from him the word he was to preach to others. But he was persecuted in carrying out his mission, he experienced abuse and attacks on his person. But in spite of this he has been true to his mission and has not rebelled against receiving the word from God nor has he hesitated to preach it to those for whom it was designed. He assented to and accepted his suffering as part of his mission, as God's will for him, and was not made ashamed because of it. In fact he is so certain that this suffering is God's will for him that he challenges his oppressors to enter into a legal contest before God (8). He is certain that God will justify him and that no one can condemn him for what he does.

Matthew 26, 14-25

Matthew makes two points in reporting this episode: Jesus' death was part of the plan of God as shown by the fact that all happened in fulfillment of the scriptures; Jesus had foreknowledge of his death and willingly accepted it out of obedience to God's will. Matthew's knowledge of the amount of money Judas received, thirty pieces of silver, does not come from historical knowledge but from Zec 11, 12. Judas' betrayal is a fulfillment of scripture and part of God's plan. Jesus' foreknowledge and acceptance of his death is brought out in the verses on the preparation of the passover meal in his statement, "my time is at hand." This same point is brought out again when he reveals that one of the twelve is going to betray him. He must die "as it is written" (24). Judas in his betrayal is fulfilling the plan of God but Jesus brings out that this does not abolish his responsibility for what he is doing. Matthew has added v. 25 to bring out once again Jesus' foreknowledge.

Reflection

When we look at a crucifix it is difficult for us to realize that Jesus is there because he wanted to be. It looks as if he were overpowered by his enemies and forced to die on the cross. Such was not the case. On one occasion the Pharisees tried to stone Jesus to death, but he easily escaped from them. On another occasion the people of his own town led him to the brink of a cliff with the intention of throwing him to death on the rocks below, but he simply turned and walked away with no one able to lay a hand on him. There are many incidents in which the enemies of Jesus tried to apprehend him to put him to death, but they were powerless to do so because, as our Lord explained, his "hour had not yet come." That hour was the time determined beforehand by his Father.

Jesus in today's gospel indicated that he knew that time set by his Father for his sacrificial death; he said, "My appointed time draws near." He also showed his foreknowledge of his death by his prediction that one of the twelve was about to betray him. But Jesus not only knew the time of his approaching death; more importantly he willingly accepted that death in loving obedience to his Father, in fulfillment of the scriptures.

In the conclusion of his presentation of himself as the Good Shepherd, our Lord said, "The Father loves me for this: that I lay down my life to take it up again. No one takes it from me; I lay it down freely" (Jn 10, 17 f). And at the Last Supper he said, "There is no greater love than this: to lay down one's life for one's friends" (Jn 15, 13). These words express the motive according to which Jesus died.

On Good Friday, or whenever we look at a crucifix, let

us realize that Jesus died because he wanted to. It was the perfect expression of his free, personal love for his Father and for us.

Alternate Reflection

Today's gospel tells how Judas finalized his plot to betray Jesus into the hands of the chief priests; in some places this day is referred to as "spy Wednesday." Though we realize that only God knows what was really in the heart of Judas, we do wonder just why he turned traitor. Was it mere avarice? The gospel does call him a thief and relates that he stole from the common purse which he held in trust for Jesus and the other apostles. But does it not seem that if he had had faith in Jesus, his faith should have conquered his greed?

The first mention of Judas as a traitor was on the occasion when Jesus promised that he would give his flesh to eat and his blood to drink. Jesus made that day of preaching on the Eucharist a supreme test of faith. When some of his own disciples walked away from him in protest that his words were hard to endure, he turned to the apostles to let them know that he demanded absolute faith as he asked, "Do you want to leave me too?" Though Peter manifested his faith in the name of the apostles, Jesus replied, "Have I not chosen you, the twelve? Yet one of you is a devil." And St. John comments, "He was speaking of Judas Iscariot . . . for he it was, though one of the twelve, who would betray him" (Jn 6, 71-72).

It was from the supper table at which Jesus instituted the Eucharist that Judas left to carry out his betrayal. The impression, at least, is left that Judas turned traitor because he had failed to pass the supreme test of faith in the Eucharist.

Tomorrow, Holy Thursday, we celebrate the institution of the Eucharist. Let us take that occasion to profess our complete faith in Jesus, and let us pray that our faith will make us loyal and faithful to him.

HOLY THURSDAY

Exodus 12, 1-8, 11-14

This is a description of the Passover rite which was celebrated every year as a memorial of what God had done in Egypt to deliver Israel: He had slaughtered the first-born of the Egyptians. This was the event which produced the intended result, the release of the Israelites from Egypt. This feast very naturally also became a memorial of the Exodus itself, the saving event of the Old Testament. The feast itself is older than the Exodus and originally was a nomadic rite in which the use of blood was important, perhaps to ward off demonic powers. At a later time this feast was "historicized," i.e., its origin was explained by the event of the first Passover night and it was given a fresh salvific meaning.

1 Corinthians 11, 23-26

The Corinthians had forgotten the full significance of the Eucharistic celebration for the **agape,** the meal commemorating the Last Supper, had become the more important part of their celebration. The 'Lord's Supper," the strictly Eucharistic part of the celebration, had fallen into the background. Abuses had even crept into the **agape** itself (17-22). Paul points out the impropriety of these abuses by recalling the real meaning of the Lord's Supper (23-34). The Lord's Supper is a sacramental re-enactment which makes present Christ's sacrifice and as such a memorial of the Lord's death and a proclamation of belief in the significance of his redemptive death and resurrection, as also of belief in his second coming. "Which is for you" signifies that Jesus died for our salvation. The "new covenant in my blood"

recalls Jeremiah's promise of a new covenant (31) and the sealing
of the Sinaitic covenant with the blood of the sacrificial victim.

John 13, 1-15

The "hour" or time for Jesus' death and his return to the
Father has now arrived. He knows what is to happen and accepts
it out of love and so gives a supreme example of his love for
those who believe. During the last meal he is having with his
disciples, he who is from God, the Son of God, performs the task
of a slave. The footwashing is followed by two explanations. In
vv. 6-11 it is explained as a prophetic action which symbolizes
the death of Jesus and manifests the humiliation involved in it.
The disciples will understand this full meaning of the footwashing only after he has been glorified. This death is necessary if
man is to be cleansed of sin and receive eternal life. The washing has also been made to refer to baptism through the vocabu-
lary used. The second explanation (12-20) presents the footwashing as an example of the humility which Christians must imitate
in their own lives.

Reflection

At this time of the year devout Jews throughout the
world continue to celebrate the Passover Supper in commemoration of God's deliverance of Israel from Egypt and
his saving of the people in the Exodus. As presented in the
New Testament, on Holy Thursday evening Jesus celebrated
the Passover Supper with his apostles. Since this liturgical
meal foreshadowed the Mass, our Lord instituted the Mass
within its framework.

At the beginning of the supper certain incidents from the
Bible were related, telling the story of the Exodus. It was
the custom for the head of the house to give an explanation
of this history and the symbolism of the meal; it was a kind
of homily. Jesus himself performed this function at the Last
Supper, and took the opportunity to elaborate on the Jewish

ritual by giving a very long sermon. Prayers of praise and thanksgiving were said, and psalms were sung.

Unleavened bread and wine were served at the meal. At one point of the meal, Jesus set aside some of the bread and wine and changed them into his body and blood as a sacred sign of his sacrifice of the next day when he would pour forth all his blood from his body in death. As the sacrifice of the lamb in Egypt saved the Jews, so the sacrifice of the Lamb of God would save the new people of God. And as the Jews partook of the sacrificial lamb, so our Lord gave his body and blood in communion to the apostles as a sacred sign of their sharing in his resurrection. Psalms were sung and the first Mass was at an end.

After Pentecost the apostles fulfilled the command of Christ, "Do this in memory of me." At first, however, they did not omit the service of the synagogue (Acts 2, 24). The synagogue service usually consisted of prayers, to which the people responded with "Amen." There were two lessons from the Old Testament, one from the Law of Moses and one from the prophets. Before and after the lessons certain interludes were sung, and then an explanation of the scripture text was given. In conclusion a sermon was preached by a rabbi.

After the break from the synagogue, this service was christianized and retained as a preparation for the Eucharist. Passages from the New Testament, then developing, were added. About the middle of the second century the basic plan of the Mass stood out clearly: lessons from the Old Testament or epistles, the gospel, homily, and prayers; all this was followed by the celebration of the Eucharist. Then over the centuries minor elements were introduced, some of which tended to obscure the basic simplicity of the Mass as instituted by Christ and handed down by the apostles.

The changes in the Mass which we have experienced since Vatican II have had for their purpose to make the Mass even more clearly a memorial of what our Lord did as carried out by the apostles and their earliest successors. For example, the prayers at the foot of the altar have been replaced by a brief penitential rite. This rite has the same purpose as the washing of the feet at the Last Supper, which, among other things, symbolized the fact that to share in the Lords' Supper the apostles had to be purified from sin. We then ask for God's mercy and praise him in the *Gloria*.

We next listen to God's word in sacred scripture and in the homily, and pray to God in the universal prayer or prayer of the faithful. This liturgy of the word obviously reflects elements of both the Last Supper and the synagogue service. In the offertory we set aside bread and wine from ordinary use, as our Lord set aside the bread and wine used in the Paschal Supper. This bread and wine become the body and blood of Christ just as at the Last Supper, as a sacred sign of his sacrifice on the cross. Then we receive Jesus in holy communion as did the apostles at the Last Supper.

Tonight on this Holy Thursday evening in a very special way we are keeping the command of Christ, "Do this in memory of me." But every Mass is the memorial of the Lord and of what he did to save us from the slavery of sin.

Alternate Reflection

On the night before he died our Lord thought of two things. He thought of heaven and ʰ ᵗhought of earth. He thought of his Father in heaven and in his human mind he contemplated his wonderful relationship with the Father: all its glory and joy and even ecstasy. What a tremendous thing to be the son of such a Father and to be about to return home! Our Lord thought of earth as well, as he turned his attention to us who live here. Since he loved us, he wanted us to share in his own joy and happiness in being the son of God. "He had loved his own in this world, and would show his love for them to the end." His prayer for us to the Father was: "That all may be one as you, Father, are in me and I in you . . . All those you gave me I would have in my company where I am . . ." (Jn 17, 21 ff).

It was in this frame of mind that our Lord instituted the Eucharist, the sign and cause of unity and love in the Church. It is true that we are united to Christ as sons of the Father by means of baptism, but that union is only a beginning, a rudimentary type of oneness. Our union with Christ grows and becomes perfect through our receiving him in holy communion. Little by little the Eucharist will transform us into Christ, enhancing and enriching and making more effective that relationship with the Father begun in baptism.

Our Lord instituted the Eucharist within the context of a family meal, the Last Supper, and we now receive the Eucharist within the context of a family meal, the Mass. A family eating together at the family table and partaking of the same food is a sign of unity. And so our unity with Christ is by its very nature a corporate reality, not an individual one only. It is impossible to come into union with Christ and through him with the Father without coming into union with the other members of God's family. Such union must find its expression in charity, love. This is why at the Last Supper Jesus gave both an example and a command of charity. His example of practical charity was one of service to the apostles: he washed their feet. His command was this: "I give you a new commandment: love one another; such as my love has been for you, so must your love be for each other" (Jn 13, 34 f).

The mysteries of this day center around the theme of the unity of the Church: in itself, in its cause which is the Eucharist, and in its application which is love. Let us through this liturgical celebration seek the grace to recognize and appreciate our oneness with Christ through the Eucharist, and let us ask for the grace to live this oneness by means of our love for one another.

GOOD FRIDAY

Isaiah 52, 13-53, 12

The fourth Servant Song. This passage is very difficult and filled with the uncertainties. But the general theme is clear. It is related that the Servant was afflicted with all kinds of suffering which made him so repugnant that he was "spurned and avoided by men." But to the surprise of all it is revealed that these sufferings were not imposed on him by God because of his own sins. He was innocent. Rather, he has been made to bear the sufferings and guilt due to the sins of others. Because he willingly and without complaint accepted these sufferings, and even surrendered himself to death, he has taken away "the sins of many," won "pardon for their offenses," and gained vindication and exaltation for himself.

Hebrews 4, 14-16; 5, 7-9

Jesus, our great high priest, has now entered the heavenly sanctuary. This should be an incentive to perseverance for he is able to sympathize with our weaknesses. He is able to sympathize because he has undergone every temptation that his people are likely to undergo, though he never succumbed, and because he has experienced the trials of human nature, especially the fear of death. In the midst of these sufferings he prayed to the Father and the Father heard him and raised him from the dead. We can, then, confidently approach the throne of God, where he is now installed, to receive all the helps we need in our time of trial for he will be merciful towards us and understand our problems. Even though he was the Son of God he learned by his experience of suffering what obedience to God involved in man's life on earth. Having been exalted as a result of his own obedience he will save all who are obedient to him.

John 18, 1-19, 42

For John the passion is the story of a victory, of Christ's glorification, in which Jesus is presented as a king, with rule over the whole world, who controls his own destiny and dies announcing that his work is done. He is the Suffering Servant and the Paschal Lamb who, at the moment of his death, gives the Spirit to mankind and brings forth the Church and the means for life in the Church, baptism and the Eucharist. John selects his material carefully, presenting only those events which have theological significance and show Christ as the Savior. He leaves out many of the indignities that Christ had to suffer since this is the story of a victory.

Reflection

In the ancient world in which our Lord lived, there was no worse death than that by crucifixion, and no penalty was more feared and despised. Consequently, the soldiers who crucified men expected them to be filled with bitterness and hatred. In fact it is related that executioners often cut out the tongue of the man to be crucified so that he could not curse them and blaspheme God.

The soldiers who crucified Christ were probably old hands at that sort of thing; it was just another day's work for them. Possibly they had seen many men die in crucifixion and in each instance they had witnessed the horror as well as the hatred in the eyes of the condemned man. They had heard his curses and his blasphemies. How amazed they must have been at what seemed to them to be serene resignation on the part of Jesus. If they had penetrated the meaning of the inscription on the cross proclaiming Jesus as King, they would have realized that his death was indeed a victory and the way to his glorification as King of all men. If they had known that Jesus was dying as victim of his own priestly sacrifice, they would have understood that far from wishing to curse on them, he was dying for the salvation of all men, and that far from blaspheming God he was offering himself in supreme worship to the Father.

Today we are here not to lament the death of Christ, even though we are in sorrow over our sins because of which Jesus died. Rather we are here to rejoice in the great victory that Jesus the King won by his death. We are here to praise and thank God that he sent his son to be the high priest who won our salvation through the worship of the cross.

Alternate Reflection

Each year in the United States we have a Memorial Day in honor of the soldiers who have died on the field of battle in the struggle against the enemies of this country so that we might be preserved in life and freedom. We have been so concerned that none of these heroes be forgotten that in Arlington National Cemetery we have erected the tomb and monument of the unknown soldier.

Today the Church throughout the whole world is having a memorial day in honor of its great hero, its soldier who died. His battle was against Satan and sin, the enemies of our salvation. His battlefield was the cross, and he died that we may have supernatural life and the freedom of the sons of God. Perhaps to many he is an unknown soldier. To others he is little known and less honored.

And yet the whole life of Christ was one of love for people, a love which reached its climax on Good Friday. On the evening before he died, Jesus said at the Last Supper, "There is no greater love than this: to lay down one's life for one's friends." On the cross Jesus freely laid down his life for our salvation. But the amazing thing is that when Jesus did die for us we were not actually his friends. We were his enemies by sin. It is truly wonderful and understandable that a man should die for his loved ones, but it is unheard of that one should die for people who have offended him and are his enemies. St. Paul wrote, "It is rare that anyone should lay down his life for a just man, though it is barely possible that for a good man someone may have the courage to die. It is precisely in this that God proves his love for us: that while we were still sinners, Christ died for us" (Rm 5, 7-9).

No one of us need wonder whether Christ loves us. Today we celebrate the memory and the reality of that great love.

EASTER VIGIL

1) **Genesis 1, 1-2, 2**

This first reading points out, in the scientific categories of the first millennium before Christ, that God is the Creator of all that exists and that he has created all things good.

2) **Genesis 22, 1-18**

Abraham receives a promise of abundant blessings from God because he has not hesitated in his obedience to the Lord.

3) **Exodus 14, 15-15, 1**

This is the account of God's deliverance of Israel from the Egyptians, the central saving event of the Old Testament.

4) **Isaiah 54, 1-4**

The Lord here tells the Israelites that even though they have abandoned him he will once again redeem them and take them back as his own people because of his great love for them.

5) **Isaiah 55, 1-11**

The Lord promises those who have abandoned him that he is ready to forgive past sins and pour out many blessings upon those who turn once again to him and listen to his word.

6) **Baruch 3, 9-15, 32-4, 4**

It is pointed out to the Israelites that they have undergone sufferings because they had abandoned God, the source of peace and wisdom, the Creator of all things. But if they will once again live according to the Law of God they will live in peace.

7) **Ezekiel 36, 16-28**

The Lord tells the people, through his prophet Ezekiel, that the suffering they have been undergoing is the result of their sins. But now he is about to deliver them once again, cleansing them from their sins and giving them a new heart and, through his spirit, the power to observe his Law. He is doing this not because of anything Israel has done but to keep his name from being profaned by the pagans.

Romans 6, 3-11

St. Paul, speaking of the effects of baptism, tells us that through baptism we have been freed from all sin and given a new life. This comes about because in baptism we are made one with Christ in his very act of dying, in which he destroyed the power of sin, as also in his resurrection in which he received a new glorified life. Being one with him in his death and resurrection we have been freed from sin and made one with Christ in his new glorified life and must now live accordingly.

(A) Matthew 28, 1-10; (B) Mark 16, 1-8; (C) Luke 24, 1-12

The point of each of these three gospels is that a person who was dead, Jesus of Nazareth, lives once again. From these three narratives it is obvious that this event has taken all by surprise, but of the fact there is no doubt. Notice that no one attempts to describe the resurrection itself.

Reflection

Tonight, in the words of St. Augustine, we celebrate "the mother of all vigils." It is a fulfillment of the Jewish vigil before Passover. The book of Exodus says, "This was a night of vigil for the Lord, as he led them out of the land of Egypt; so on this same night all the Israelites must keep a vigil for the Lord throughout their generations" (Ex 12, 42). Among the Israelites the yearly vigil of Passover was a commemoration of the most glorious event of their past, their liberation from the slavery of Egypt. But it also looked to the future in expectation of the coming of the Messiah.

The Christian vigil is, as with all liturgical functions, past, present, and future in its outlook. St. Augustine wrote, "Our annual celebration is not simply a commemoration of a past event; it implies a present action on our part, which we accomplish by our life of faith and of which this vigil is the symbol. The entire course of time is in fact one long night during which the Church keeps watch, waiting for the return of the Lord, waiting "until he comes.'" There is a very ancient belief, and St. Jerome says that it is apostolic in origin, that Christ will come in glory at the *parousia* in the night of the Easter vigil.

Tonight, then, in faith we have kept vigil, recalling the saving death of our Lord and his glorious resurrection. We have renewed our baptism, which was our original sharing in the death and resurrection of Christ. That baptism gave us the power to participate in the Mass, which makes his sacrificial death and victorious resurrection a reality among us.

Tonight we should make a special effort to join with Christ enthusiastically in the loving offering of himself to the Father during the Eucharistic Prayer, and let us receive the glorious body of the resurrected Christ in a spirit of faith and joy.

The deep spiritual happiness that should be ours tonight is not something we can explain or even express. There is, however, one word repeated many times in the liturgy, a word that is meant to give voice to our almost inexpressible happiness, a word that should be in our hearts as well as on our lips as we wait for Christ to come again in glory, and that one word is "Alleluia!"

INDEX TO BIBLICAL PASSAGES

16:19-31 — Th of 2
18:9-14 — Sat of 3
John
    4:5-42 — Opt of 3
    4:43-54 — Mon of 4
    5:1-3a; 5-16 — Tu of 4
    5:17-30 — Wed of 4
    5:31-47 — Th of 4
    7:1-2; 10; 25-30 — Fr of 4
    7:40-53 — Sat of 4
    8:1-11 — Mon of 5
    8:12-20 — Mon of 5
    8:21-30 — Tu of 5
    8:31-42 — Wed of 5
    8:51-59 — Th of 5

    9:1-41 — Opt of 4
    10:31-42 — Fr of 5
    11:1-45 — Opt of 5
    11:45-57 — Sat of 5
    12:1-11 — Mon of H. W.
    13:1-15 — Holy Th
    13:21-33; 36-38 — Tu of H. W.
    18:1-19; 42 — Good Fr
1 Corinthians
    11:23-26 — Holy Th
2 Corinthians
    5:20-6; 2 — Ash Wed
Hebrews
    4:14-16; 5:7-9 — Good Fr